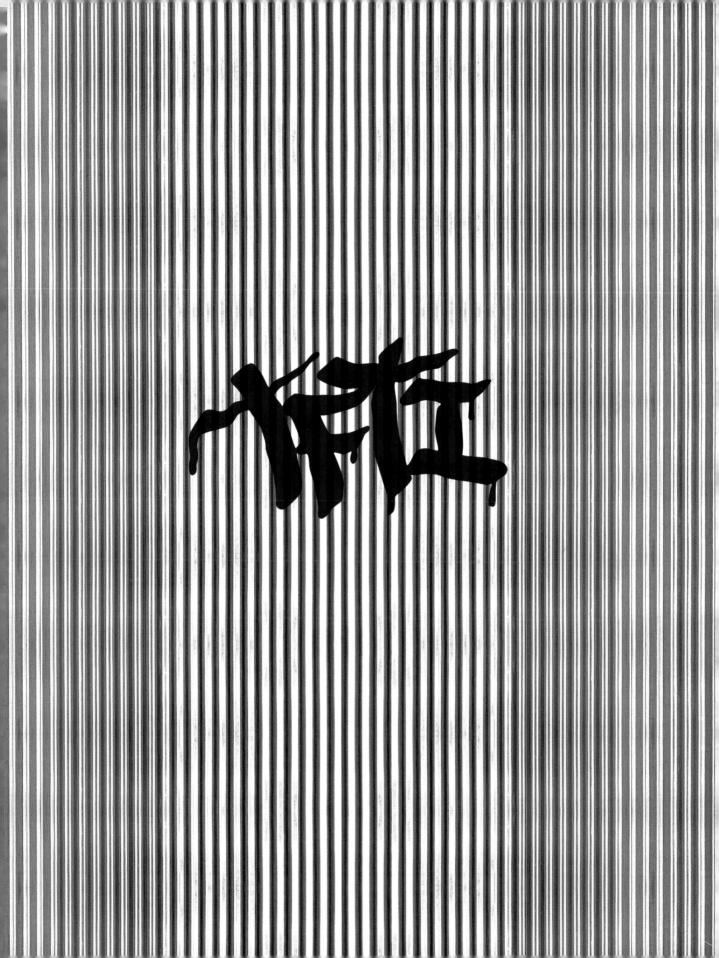

Filipino- and Cajun-Inspired Recipes for the Smoker and Grill

BACKYARD BBQ WITH FIRE AND SPICE

TONY RAMIREZ
Creator of TFTI BBQ

HARVARD
COMMON
PRESS

Quarto.com

© 2025 Quarto Publishing Group USA Inc.
Text © 2025 Antonio Efren Ramirez

First Published in 2025 by The Harvard Common Press,
an imprint of The Quarto Group,
100 Cummings Center, Suite 265-D, Beverly, MA 01915, USA.
T (978) 282-9590 F (978) 283-2742

The Harvard Common Press titles are also available at discount for retail, wholesale, promotional, and bulk purchase. For details, contact the Special Sales Manager by email at specialsales@quarto.com or by mail at The Quarto Group, Attn: Special Sales Manager, 100 Cummings Center, Suite 265-D, Beverly, MA 01915, USA.

29 28 27 26 25   1 2 3 4 5

ISBN: 978-0-7603-9452-6

Digital edition published in 2025
eISBN: 978-0-7603-9453-3

Library of Congress Cataloging-in-Publication Data
Names: Ramirez, Tony, author.
Title: The backyard BBQ with fire and spice : Filipino- and Cajun-inspired
  recipes for the smoker and grill / Tone Ramirez.
Other titles: Backyard barbeque with fire and spice
Description: Beverly, MA, USA : Harvard Common Press, an imprint of the
  Quarto Group, 2025. | Includes index.
Identifiers: LCCN 2024044425 (print) | LCCN 2024044426 (ebook) | ISBN
  9780760394526 (board) | ISBN 9780760394533 (ebook)
Subjects: LCSH: Cooking, Philippine. | Cooking, Cajun. | Barbecuing. |
  LCGFT: Cookbooks.
Classification: LCC TX724.5.P5 R358 2025 (print) | LCC TX724.5.P5 (ebook)
  | DDC 641.5/784--dc23/eng/20241029
LC record available at https://lccn.loc.gov/2024044425
LC ebook record available at https://lccn.loc.gov/2024044426

Design and Page Layout: Cindy Samargia Laun
Photography: Smoke & Vine LLC, except Tony Ramirez on page 5 and endpapers

Printed in China

This book is lovingly dedicated to my beloved mother, Patricia Ramirez. She was the heart and soul of our family, a woman whose strength, love, and incredible spirit touched everyone who knew her. Her cooking was legendary—a blend of her Cajun and Filipino heritage, crafted with her own unique flair. It was truly the best, and anyone who had the privilege of tasting her food would agree.

My mother was a stay-at-home wife to my amazing father, Efren Ramirez Sr., who was a cook in the Navy. Despite her busy life, she poured her heart into every meal, creating dishes that were more than just food—they were a connection to our roots and a testament to her boundless love for us.

I never cooked alongside her, as that kitchen was her domain, and she ruled it with a beautiful, strong, and sometimes strict hand. But I watched, I learned, and I carry her lessons with me every day. This book is a manifestation of those lessons, a way to honor her legacy and keep her memory alive.

My mother was an avid cookbook collector, and this one is written with her in mind—to be added to the collection she cherished so much. I wish she were here to see it, but I know she's with me on every page.

Thank you, Mom, for everything. I miss you more than words can express.

I love you.

PARTY FOOD 129

SMOKE IT 165

INTRODUCTION

The enticing smell of delicious BBQ on a grill or smoker always draws a crowd.

I learned that early on in my BBQ journey. I grew up in a tight community, and it was the rare weekend that we weren't at my uncle's house for a cookout. We lived right across the bay from San Francisco in Hayward. My part of California has always had the perfect weather for long afternoons outside. Some of my happiest memories are from large backyard cookouts with all of us cousins running around while the adults just relaxed. Those were epically happy times because BBQ is more than food; it's a magnet that draws people together and makes every occasion—even a plain-old weekend—an event to remember.

When it came time to man the grill myself, I jumped at the chance. As I settled into my own home and started my own family, I kept that happy ball rolling. I invited friends and family to my table. When I became president of my local car club, I hosted all the group meetings at my place, cooking big spreads for all the members.

Every time I'd try out a new recipe, one friend or another would find out and text me "TFTI," which meant "Thanks for the invite." It was a friendly little inside joke.

My cookouts grew and grew, and my collection of recipes increased. Every gathering was the opportunity to try out something new: unique flavor combos; a different type of smoking with a new kind of wood; or a whole new prep method. It's no surprise that those early experiences didn't just feed my friends and family—they fed my passion and gave me a way to express my creativity.

Looking back, it was bound to become a business. It was fate that I would name the business TFTI. It was just a matter of following my heart, really, and listening to what people wanted. I've always found it incredibly rewarding to create dope new recipes that are completely different from what people might expect of a backyard BBQ. The smell of BBQ still means family, fun, and love to me.

The truth is, BBQ has never been just about the food. It's an event, a community, and the straw that stirs the drink. BBQ takes time. That's hanging out time, with music playing and people laughing. More than anything, BBQ (at least the way I do it) is a reason to connect with your tribe and spend quality time with the people who mean the most to you. It's memories in the making. The spirit of TFTI is to welcome everyone with an appetite and a healthy fear of missing out.

That's what BBQ has always meant to me, and it's what I've tried to capture in this book.

A Way of Living

I'm dedicated to BBQ. It's not just how I make a living; it's how I live. BBQ is a lifestyle focused on food, friends, fun, and mixing all those things together.

My cooking style is a tribute to my late mother, a devoted stay-at-home mom who absolutely loved cooking for her family. She was a Cajun Filipino straight out of Louisiana, and it came through in everything she cooked. My dad is Filipino and has the same passion for good, filling food. He was a cook in the Navy and no stranger to making delicious meals for lots of people. But once he started building a life together with my mom, she made it clear that the kitchen was hers (LOL).

I lean into blending those two rich culinary traditions—Cajun and Filipino—in my BBQ recipes. In that sense, everything I make is a homage to my parents and the love they put into their food and our home. I hope the recipes in this book become the same for you and yours.

BBQ AND SMOKING MY WAY

BBQ is all about fun. It's also an adventure in creativity and an incredible way to express yourself. There are a nearly endless number of spice and flavor combinations to explore. You can mix and match prep and cooking techniques, the type of wood or charcoal you're using, and temperatures from low to high. The goal isn't to do it the right way because there is no such thing as the "right" BBQ. There's only the BBQ that works best for you, your backyard, and your people.

The only way to really figure out what that means is to experiment. That's what I've been doing ever since I bought my first grill.

Early on, I devoured YouTube videos, books, and whatever advice I could find. Experimentation was always my best teacher. I discovered it pays to be fearless in trying out new techniques and recipes. After all, what do you have to lose? One of the great things about BBQ is that even the accidents and mistakes usually taste pretty good.

Through all that trial and error, I carved out a style that's all mine and distinctly TFTI. I think of it as "fusion BBQ." It's a mash-up of Cajun spice blends, Filipino ingredients, fresh flavors, and a mix of traditional smoking, grilling, and open-pit techniques.

As you go through the book and pick the recipes that speak to you, don't be afraid to put your own spin on things. Mix it up. Make it yours. That's what I did. You'll know you nailed it when it's money. "Money" means too good to put into words. You take a bite, chew it, and it's just . . . money. It's that big payday of flavor, texture, and heat.

STOCKING THE PANTRY

Like all Pitmasters, I turn to certain spices, flavors, and products again and again. I stay stocked up because the products are so adaptable and useful that I never want to be caught short. (I've included a Resources section of my favorite brands for these ingredients at the end of this book.)

Spice blends. Yeah, you can make your own, but there are companies and pros out there who do nothing but develop incredible spice-forward rubs and mixes to create different and unique flavor blends. The benefit of using these prepared products is consistency. If the flavor blows you away, you know it will be the same every time you use it.

I made a special spice drawer to keep jars of my favorites organized and close at hand. Using prepared spice mixes and rubs makes life a lot easier. Even so, I've included generic substitutions in recipes where the flavors don't absolutely hinge on a particular product. I'd still urge you to try the products I mention because they bring something special to the party. It's also a good idea to always be on the hunt for new products that will take your flavors in unique directions.

A word to the wise about hot peppers and spices. Don't mistake heat for flavor. "Hot and spicy" is a preference. Me, I'm not about blowing out my guests' taste buds. The heat in my recipes is always in service of the flavors.

Special ingredients. The essentials aside, always look for what will work best for your BBQ. For instance, honey is a simple, common ingredient in BBQ sauces and marinades. The question is, which honey? There is a world of flavor differences between clover honey, lavender honey, manuka honey, and other varieties. This one ingredient is way more than just a sweetener. That kind of variety is why I'm always on the hunt for new ingredients that will put an interesting twist on my next recipe. The best place to look for those is a well-stocked local Asian market. That's where you'll find the more unusual ingredients in my recipes and where you can discover interesting, tasty gems hiding in plain sight down just about any aisle.

THE BIG GEAR

Don't get carried away with your equipment when you first start your BBQ adventure. You can do a ton of BBQ on a simple OG Weber kettle grill. That's how I started. It may be a little challenging to cook everything you want to try, but you can actually grill and smoke with even a simple, budget, direct-fire model. Once you're ready, look for a higher-end unit with options that will make life easier or that's dedicated to one type of cooking, such as a smoker. However, better, more specialized equipment won't mean much until you've developed the skills and knowledge necessary to really take advantage of the technology.

Grill. The most popular are charcoal-fired kettle grills. Super useful and inexpensive, they're simple to use whether you're cooking over direct or indirect heat. Gas units are a step up, with propane-fired burners that provide even, controllable heating, easier cleanup, and extras like side burners for cooking in pots and pans. Electric grills are less popular, but offer the same benefits as a gas model. The downside is that they have to be placed near an outdoor outlet. *Kamado* grills are egg-shaped imports from Japan, with ceramic shells that offer superior insulation and incredibly even heating. They're efficient, heavy, and expensive. The type and size of grill you choose depends on your budget, how many people you typically cook for, and the fuel source that gives you the flavors you're after (gas grilling leaves virtually no flavor behind, while lump charcoal imparts a distinctive flavor). Wheels or casters are a must because sooner or later you'll need to move your grill.

Smoker. Shopping for a smoker starts with choosing a fuel type: electric, gas, or charcoal-and-wood. Electric models are simple to operate, with an electric coil that heats wood chips or pellets. Air flow can be tricky, but otherwise they are as easy to use as your kitchen stove. Gas-fired smokers operate in much the same way but have a gas burner. They are also easy to operate but usually won't go below 250°F (120°C), so smoking at very low temperatures for long periods isn't really an option. Each type creates slightly different flavors and smoke effects than a more traditional offset charcoal-and-wood smoker will.

Both electric and gas units are typically "vertical" smokers, with the cooking chamber stacked right over the heat and fuel source. That makes it hard to sear the surface of meat cuts, but you can heat an upside-down cast-iron skillet in the smoker to sear as needed.

The type of wood product is the next consideration. Pellet smokers are the easiest to use and give you a lot of control (they're considered the most beginner-friendly). They use compressed wood pellets rather than wood chips or chunks, and most pellet smokers can be programmed to run without supervision. They are, however, pricier than other types. Some cooks might disagree, but I find pellets don't impart as rich a flavor as smoking with wood logs and chunks. Traditional charcoal-and-wood smokers are heated by the namesake fuels and are manually operated. You'll need to tend the unit and monitor the fire, and all of that takes a certain amount of expertise, but they offer the ultimate smoking experience.

Beyond those decisions, you'll choose from among three different smoker construction styles. Offset includes a separate smoke chamber where the wood is heated off to one side of the cooking chamber. These are the traditional style and what pros use. Vertical smokers stack the cooking platform right over the heat source. Grill-format smokers are essentially a grill with enough room for indirect heat and smoke. Signs of quality are same regardless: a thick metal shell, portability (wheels), a tight lid seal and abundant body insulation, a nice range of options, and safety features like anti-tip technology. Price and warranty are the best signs of quality and longevity.

I want to give an honorable mention to a newer technology that I'm using with some of my quicker-cooking recipes. It's a combination air fryer, grill, and smoker in one unit. It's really only applicable for smaller cuts, but can be a shortcut when the recipe calls for more than one cooking method.

Chamber vacuum sealer. This isn't a must-have, but it makes your life and cooking a lot easier. I use mine all the time. Like the basic home vacuum sealer, a chamber vacuum sealer will remove all the air from a freezer bag, allowing you to keep leftovers in long-term storage without losing flavor. That's important for anyone who regularly grills or smokes for large backyard gatherings—you're bound to have extras, and you don't want all that deliciousness to go to waste.

More importantly to me, though, are the range of extra settings on a chamber vacuum sealer. Because it has a "chamber" cavity into which you can place bags of food, the unit can marinate and brine much more quickly than normal. Pressurizing forces marinade into the protein, so that two rounds of 90-second marination in the chamber vacuum sealer equals about a day of marination in the refrigerator, with virtually no difference in the final flavors. I have two little kids, so any time I save in prep is time I can spend with them.

THE SMALL GEAR

These are just as important when it comes to cooking BBQ. The proper hand tools make the whole process quicker, easier, and more controllable.

Thermometer. This is the most important tool for perfect BBQ time after time. If you don't know the internal temperature of your food, you're flying blind. Some cooks use a point-and-shoot digital thermometer, but that's not good enough because success hinges on *internal* temperature. Buy a probe thermometer. A basic instant-read digital probe meat thermometer is inexpensive and will work well for most purposes, but it may require poking the protein several times before it is ready to be pulled off the grill. That can lead to the unacceptable loss of super tasty juices. That's why I use wireless probes. You simply stick the probe into the protein before you start cooking and pull it out when you're done. It couldn't be easier. You monitor the temperature with a reader that is sold with the probe (mine are smart probes that transmit readings right to my phone). Because I cook multiple cuts at one time, I bought a set.

Skewers. Thanks to my Filipino influence, I grill a lot of skewered meats. Metal skewers are essential. They hold even heavy loads, are a breeze to clean, and never deform. I'd recommend buying double skewers (with two tines rather than one) because they make it easy to thread even odd-shaped proteins securely onto the skewer.

The TFTI Guide to Charcoal and Wood

The charcoal or wood you choose for grilling and smoking have a tremendous impact on the flavor of your BBQ. They also determine how easy cleanup will be and how much you'll spend.

Briquettes

Charcoal briquettes	These are made with sawdust and other fillers; are inexpensive, fast burning, and messy; and are good for "low-and-slow" cooking (low temperature and long cook time) thanks to consistent temperature when burning. Avoid "match light" products with lighter fluid because they give food a chemical taste.
Lump briquettes	These are formed from whole wood burned in low oxygen; have a cleaner flavor and more pleasant smoke; are often used for hot-and-fast grilling; and are more expensive. Oak is the most common, but it's available in pecan, apple, and hickory, as well.

Wood

Apple	Applewood has a sweet, light, fruity flavor that really shines when used for pork, chicken, or fish. It burns evenly and lasts, so it's a good value for the money.
Cherry	Cherrywood has a delicate and sweet flavor. It's best for pork and beef, where you don't want the smoking to overpower the spice rub or marinade flavors.
Hickory	Hickory's intense, sweet, baconlike flavor can overpower some proteins. Split logs are good for long smoking, whereas chunks and chips work best for shorter smoke times. It's especially good for skin-on turkey, game, and beef and darkens the surface more than other woods do.
Maple	Maple has a light, sweet flavor and pleasant-smelling smoke. It's an excellent all-around choice that's good for any protein, as well as for smoking cheese and veggies.
Mesquite	Mesquite imparts a powerful, spicy flavor, is very smoky when burned, and burns quickly. It can impart a bitterness, which is why it's often used in a mix with other woods. It's best used with red meats and pork.
Oak	Oak is the most common, with a strong flavor that's best suited for red meat. It's less costly than other types of wood. Choose either post oak or live oak.
Pecan	Pecan has a strong, sweet, nutty flavor, is easy to start, and is long-burning. It's great for beef, but also good for game and poultry.

Utensils and cookware. There are certain tools of the trade I couldn't do without. A sturdy spatula is key (never use a fork for moving BBQ food or you'll bleed precious juices). Some Pitmasters use wood spatulas because they don't transmit heat, so they won't burn your hand; I use a heavy-duty metal version with a rubber handle to prevent burns. I have a quality cast-iron skillet and cast-iron saucepot that I use every day. Invest a little money to buy quality utensils, pots, and pans, and you'll be making your BBQ life a whole lot easier.

BBQ THE TFTI WAY

Learning the basics of BBQ sets the stage for you to express your cooking creativity. Once you understand the fundamentals, you can start to build your skills and tackle more challenging techniques and recipes and even create your own dishes from scratch.

Proper Prep

BBQ recipes almost always require prepping whatever you're cooking before it goes over the heat. This can be just as important as the cooking itself and can make or break the flavors in the final dish.

Dry rubs. Rubs are dried blends of spices, herbs, zests, and other ingredients. They are meant to add flavor, create a crust on the protein's surface, and seal in juices. Rubs should be pressed into the surface of the meat or poultry. I tend to use "binders" to help my rubs adhere. A binder is any slightly sticky liquid that can itself add a little bit of flavor. Nut or vegetable oils and soy sauce are examples. You don't absolutely have to have a binder under a rub, but it really helps hold the rub in place.

Marinades. A marinade serves a similar role to a rub. It infuses the protein with flavor, ensures tenderness, and keeps the flesh moist. Most marinades include an acid such as citrus juice or vinegar, which helps the flavors penetrate the protein's surface. Marination takes time, usually the longer, the better—24 to 48 hours is common—unless you're using a chamber vacuum sealer on the marination setting. That can cut hours down to minutes.

Brine. Think of brines as simpler, salt-based marinades. The most basic brine is just saltwater. The purpose is to weaken the structure of the protein, which makes the food more fall-apart tender and locks in juiciness. Brines naturally add a slight amount of saltiness. Like marinades, brines work their magic over time.

Many marinades, brines, and even leftover rubs can be reserved and used as the bases for sauces. This is a great way to exploit flavor-rich ingredients that otherwise might be drained off and discarded. Please note that if the marinade was used for uncooked meats or seafood, it must be brought up to a rolling boil to a temperature of at least 165°F (74°C) before it can be reused or repurposed in order to protect against harmful bacteria.

Food Handling Safety

Proper food prep focuses on safety first. That means cooking proteins to at least the minimal internal temperature recommended by the FDA and other experts (see the recommendations on page 26). But prep should also be done carefully to eliminate any risk of food-borne pathogens. The last thing you want is for your BBQ to make your guests sick.

This is most important with chicken. Raw chicken can contain some nasty microbes. It's a good idea to wear latex gloves when prepping chicken (I use them whenever I'm handling food). Limit splashing when washing raw chicken to avoid spreading any germs. Thoroughly wash all utensils and surfaces that come into contact with the chicken using hot water and dish soap.

Never keep raw proteins in the same refrigerator drawer or container with dairy products or vegetables. Store them at the bottom of the refrigerator to prevent cross-contamination. They should be refrigerated in their own containers or wrapped securely in plastic wrap. Make sure your refrigerator is cool enough (below 40°F, or 4°C) for properly storing raw proteins, especially if you're marinating or brining for long periods.

Indirect vs. Direct Cooking

The two ways to cook BBQ are indirect or direct heat. Start with this: Heat rises, and it likes to rise straight upward. Put food directly in its path, and the food cooks quickly in the most intense heat possible. Place the food off to the side, and the food is exposed to more disperse heat that circulates *around* the food, cooking it more slowly.

Direct heat cooks food quickly, but it also cooks the outside quicker than the inside. That's why most BBQ Pitmasters use direct heat for smaller and thinner foods and cuts. Think chicken wings, flank steak, or thin-cut pork chops. Direct heat right over the source is great for charring surfaces without overcooking the interior. The food needs to be flipped more often, and pulling something off the heat is an easy way to slow down the cooking speed and finish off the process. Direct heat is used to cook on a grill, in a pan placed right over the source, or with food (usually wrapped in foil or other covering) placed right on top of the coals. Direct heat is the most common method of cooking.

Cooking with indirect heat involves placing the food near the source, but off to the side so that it is exposed to ambient radiant heat. The process is trickier because the food cooks at a less predictable pace. This type of cooking is great for larger, thicker, and more substantial foods and cuts. It's especially effective for breaking down thickly marbled meats to make them juicier and more tender. Typically, indirect heat requires much more time and monitoring than direct-heat cooking does. Smoking is always indirect.

Making Fire (and Smoke)

Setting up a grill, smoker, or open pit requires knowing how to build and manage the fire and the heat coming from it. Master the heat and you master the BBQ.

Grilling. Like many BBQ cooks, I use a charcoal chimney to start my grill fires. The chimney has been around for decades and couldn't be simpler. It's a basic metal tube with a grate on one end and a wood handle attached to the side. Start the fire by piling the amount of charcoal you'll need for the heat you want to generate into the chimney (completely full usually translates to medium-high heat in a basic kettle grill; you can always do two chimney loads if you're cooking over very high heat). Use more if your grill is larger than average. Stand the chimney on the grill grate on top of a starter like crumpled-up newspaper or wood shavings. Never use lighter fluid or your food will taste of chemicals. Light the starter and leave the chimney until the top coals glow red. Pour the coals into the base of the grill in an even layer (or off to one side if you're cooking with indirect heat).

Some cooks add wood chunks or chips to the chimney when starting the coals. I add them on top of the coals after I spread them out, but before I start grilling.

Smoking. Firing up a smoker is easy if you have a gas, electric, or pellet smoker. Put the wood chips or pellets over the heat source or into the pellet feeder, set the desired temperature, and let it go. A more traditional offset smoker requires starting the charcoal and wood (or just wood) in the smoking chamber. Once the fire comes up to temperature, begin smoking the protein in the cook chamber. You'll need to monitor the temperature, adding wood as the fires goes down and the smoke chamber cools. Traditional smoking requires a lot of attention to both temperature and cook time, and the fire needs to be carefully maintained. It's a lot to master, and that's why backyard cooks who are new to smoking usually start with the easier-to-use pellet smoker.

Open-pit cooking. Hanging or leaning meat over a firepit can be a fantastic way to cook with indirect or direct heat. I use the "log cabin" method to create a fire in my pit, and it's just like it sounds. Stack the split wood logs as you would build the four walls of a log cabin, each layer perpendicular to the one below, overlapping at the ends. The fire starter and wood chips are piled in the center of the cabin. This creates an even heat across the fire, unlike the "teepee" formation campers often use to make a campfire. There are many hanging devices you can buy to support even heavy cuts over the fire, but it's just as easy to make your own. The important thing is to allow for adjustment, so that you can hang the protein higher or lower, depending on how quick and intensely you want to cook it.

A big added bonus to pit cooking is that it creates a vibe. The food isn't hidden, and your guests connect with it right away. The smell and appeal of the BBQ is there right in front of you. Open-pit cooking naturally inspires people to hang out around the pit and socialize while they stare into the coals. Some of my favorite times were spent around an open pit with cousins and friends in a circle, just talking, listening to music, and drinking a beer.

Measuring Temperature

There's no substitute for knowing the exact internal temperature of whatever you're cooking. The only way to determine that is by using a thermometer (you'll find a description of different types on page 18). Stick the probe into the thickest part of whatever you're cooking. Make sure it's not touching bone or anywhere close to a bone.

The TFTI Doneness Chart

These are my guidelines for final temps on various proteins, but some sources list different temperatures. Keep in mind that you have to account for carryover cooking as the protein rests (the temperature continues to increase for a short time). Your experience with any given cut may also vary. What you consider rare, someone else might think of as blue.

FDA recommends:

Beef, veal, lamb meat cuts	145°F (63°C)
Ground beef, veal, lamb	160°F (71°C)
Poultry (chicken, turkey, duck)	165°F (74°C)
Fish	145°F (63°C)

TFTI recommends (for beef steak and roasts):

Rare	120°F to 125°F (49°C to 52°C)
Medium	130°F to 135°F (54°C to 57°C)
Well	140°F to 145°F (60°C to 63°C)

* Bridge measures like "medium rare" fall between the listed temperature ranges.

Carryover Cooking and Resting Your BBQ

It sounds counterintuitive, but don't cook your BBQ all the way to the target temp. All proteins should "rest" for a certain period when they come off the grill or are pulled out of the smoker. During that time, juices saturate and settle, ensuring that they don't run out when you cut the food. More importantly, the temperature continues to rise slightly even after the meat, poultry, or fish is removed from the heat source. This is called "carryover cooking," and it has to be part of your timing calculations. For instance, a 1 inch (2.5 cm)-thick steak cooked to rare continues to cook for 4 to 5 minutes after you take it off the grill. If you want it truly rare, you need to pull it off early.

I rest whatever I've cooked fairly close to the grill or smoker. Some cooks cover food that is resting, but I just keep mine out of the breeze and off cold surfaces that would stop the carryover cooking process too quickly. The larger, thicker, and denser the protein, the longer it should rest. Most BBQ recipes, including most of mine, list a suggested resting period. After you've worked with them awhile, you'll get a sense of how long you need to rest a chicken breast (5 to 10 minutes) as opposed to a brisket (15 to 20 minutes), and then you can incorporate those times into your own recipes.

That may all seem like a mountain of information to master but don't let it overwhelm you. The best way to build skills no matter what kind of outdoor cooking you're doing is to actually prepare the food. So now that you've set up your kitchen and equipment and are familiar with the basics, it's time to start working on some delicious BBQ!

FILIPINO FAVORITES

There is a long tradition of BBQ in the Philippines. They call it *Pinoy* BBQ, and the style leans heavy in the direction of pork, chicken, and seafood. That's because it's an island nation, so fishing and raising chicken and pigs are all a lot easier and cheaper than cattle ranching. However, there are several classic Filipino beef dishes too. I've included

It's grab-and-go food that you can eat walking around and part of the culture that I just love. That visit taught me a lot about my heritage and even more about the wonders of Filipino BBQ.

Whatever your choice of protein, Filipino BBQ has you covered. The flavors are unique, but they translate to anything you're putting over a fire or coals. Traditionally, the dishes are either grilled or skewered and spit-cooked over an open fire. I adapt them to my own style, which sometimes includes smoking.

Filipino BBQ centers around marinades that

SPICY FILIPINO BBQ CHICKEN SKEWERS

YIELD: 2 to 4 servings — PREP: 20 minutes — MARINATING: 3 to 24 hours — COOK: 40 minutes

Let me tell you, there is a whole world worth exploring in the aisles of a well-stocked Asian market (or in a crunch, on Amazon). One of the many gems you'll find is spicy banana ketchup, sometimes labeled "Spicy Banana Sauce." It's kind of amazing how a simple unique condiment like this can really round out the flavors in a marinade or basting sauce. I experiment all the time with ingredients like that, especially when cooking chicken because it's such a flavor sponge.

3 pounds (1.4 kg) boneless, skinless chicken breasts

For both the Marinade and the Basting Sauce

1½ cups (355 ml) soy sauce

1 cup (235 ml) lemon juice

1½ cups (360 g) spicy banana ketchup

½ cup (115 g) packed light brown sugar

¼ cup (24 g) garlic powder

2 teaspoons freshly ground black pepper

¼ cup (72 g) salt

1½ cups (355 ml) lemon or lime soda

1. Cut the chicken into bite-size chunks. In a large bowl, combine all the marinade and basting sauce ingredients except for the soda and mix well. Divide into two equal portions and set aside half the mixture for basting. Stir the soda into the marinade portion.

2. Add the chicken to the marinade and toss to coat. Cover and refrigerate overnight if possible, but for at least 3 hours.

3. Prepare your grill with applewood, removing the rack so that the coals are exposed. Spear the chicken on metal skewers (wood skewers can burn or even catch fire) and lay the skewers across the bowl of the grill, 6 to 8 inches (15 to 20 cm) above the flame. You can also use a rotisserie rack if you have one, but only if you can get the skewers close enough to the coals.

4. Grill for a total of 3 to 5 minutes per side. Turn the skewers regularly, basting with the basting sauce after each turn. Keep on this; the chicken can burn if left on one side too long. Grill the skewers until a nice char develops and the internal temperature reaches 165°F (74°C).

5. Remove the skewers from the heat and let rest for 3 to 5 minutes or until cool enough to touch. Serve and enjoy.

TOCINO PULLED-PORK SANDWICH

YIELD: 8 sandwiches — PREP: 30 minutes — MARINATING: 24 to 48 hours — COOK: 7 hours

It's hard to beat the simple and satisfying pleasure of a well-made pulled-pork sandwich like this one. Portable, delicious, and filling, how could you go wrong? Make sure it's the best it can be by buying a quality pork shoulder. They don't put grades on pork cuts like they do on beef, so you need to shop smart. A premium pork shoulder will be well marbled with clean, pearl-white fat and meat that is much darker pink than pork loin. Once you have the meat, there's not much more to the sandwich. If you aren't down with the pickles I put on mine, you can always go with more traditional coleslaw or just drench it in your favorite BBQ sauce and leave well enough alone.

For the Pork Shoulder

1 whole boneless pork shoulder (2 pounds, or 910 g)

½ cup (1½ ounces, or 43 grams) SPG (salt, pepper, garlic) seasoning blend of choice

½ cup (96 g) pork rub of choice

For the Marinade

1 cup (235 ml) cane vinegar

½ cup (120 ml) soy sauce

1 cup (225 g) packed light brown sugar

3 cans (8 ounces, or 235 ml) 100 percent mango juice

2 tablespoons (28 g) kosher salt

2 tablespoons (16 g) coarse ground black pepper

2 tablespoons (20 g) minced garlic

1 tablespoon (15 g) rice flour

5 to 6 drops of natural red food coloring (optional)

For the Sandwiches

8 large eggs

8 brioche buns

½ cup (115 g) mayonnaise

½ cup (78 g) hamburger dill pickle chips

(CONTINUED)

1. Slice the pork shoulder into four evenly thick steaks. In a large bowl with a lid, combine the marinade ingredients and mix thoroughly. Submerge the steaks, cover, and refrigerate for at least 24 and preferably 48 hours.

2. Prepare the smoker with hickory or your favorite wood over high heat (about 300°F, or 150°C). Remove the steaks from the marinade and pat them dry (reserve the marinade in the fridge).

3. Season the pork all over with SPG seasoning, then a liberal coating of pork rub. Insert a wireless meat thermometer in one of the pork steaks and smoke the steaks for 2 to 4 hours or until the internal temperature reaches 180°F (82°C) and a nice bark has formed on the pork.

4. Transfer the pork to a large roasting pan (but small enough to fit in the smoker) and cover with the reserved marinade. Seal tightly with aluminum foil and return to the smoker. Smoke for about 2 hours more or until the internal temperature reaches 200°F (93°C).

5. Remove the pork from the pan, drain, and set aside to rest for 2 hours. After it's fully rested, shred the pork. It should be easy to pull apart with your hands, or you can use a large fork.

6. Heat a nonstick skillet over medium heat. Gently crack an egg into the skillet, cook until the whites are nearly set, and then flip the egg and cook for about 15 seconds more, just until the yolk sets up.

7. Toast the brioche buns. Spread about 1 tablespoon (14 g) of mayonnaise on a bottom half. Top with a few dill chips, a generous mound of the shredded pork, and then the egg. Cover with the top of the bun. Repeat with remaining sandwich makings and enjoy!

SMOKED CHICKEN ARROZ CALDO

YIELD: 4 servings —— PREP: 20 minutes —— COOK: 40 minutes

Arroz Caldo is justly famous as one of the best Filipino comfort dishes (it basically translates to "rice broth" or "rice stew"). The original includes chicken pieces cooked in broth that leans heavy on ginger. Filipino grandmothers use it like Jewish grandmothers use chicken soup, prescribing it for just about any sickness. I decided to put my own BBQ spin on it, while still honoring the original. Do you live in an apartment but want that BBQ goodness? No sweat. This dish can be made on the stove in a pinch. Traditionally made and served with a sliced hardboiled egg, dress it up whatever way makes sense for you.

2 pounds (910 g) chicken wings

Salt and pepper to taste

2 tablespoons (24 g) BBQ rub of choice

2 tablespoons (28 ml) olive oil

½ large white onion, peeled and diced

6 cloves garlic, peeled, crushed, and coarsely chopped

1 piece (2 inches, or 5 cm) fresh ginger, peeled and sliced thin

1 tablespoon (15 ml) fish sauce

5½ cups (1.3 L) chicken broth

1 cup (195 g) white rice

Pinch of saffron (optional)

1 green onion, chopped (optional)

1 large lemon, sliced (optional)

Crispy fried garlic (optional)

1 large hardboiled egg, peeled and sliced (optional)

1. Prepare your grill with your favorite briquettes to high heat or about 400°F (200°C).

2. In a large bowl, season the wings with salt, pepper, and the BBQ rub. Toss until completely coated and then transfer the wings to the grill. Grill the wings, flipping them frequently, for 12 to 15 minutes or until they are cooked through with dark brown skin and a slight char. When they're done, transfer them to a plate and set aside.

3. Heat the olive oil in a cast-iron Dutch oven over the hot coals in the grill. Add the onion, garlic, and ginger. Cook them until fragrant, about 5 minutes.

4. Add the chicken wings to the Dutch oven and stir for about 1 minute. Pour in the fish sauce, mix well, and cook for another 2 minutes.

5. Add the chicken broth and rice. Stir well and bring to a boil. Cover and transfer the pot from the coals to the grill grate. Simmer for 10 minutes while stirring regularly to prevent the rice from sticking to the bottom of the pot.

(CONTINUED)

6. Season everything with salt, pepper, and the saffron, if you're using it (the saffron gives the dish the beautiful yellow color of the Filipino original). Stir again to combine. Cook for 2 to 3 minutes more.

7. Add some applewood chunks to the coals. Remove the lid on the pot and close the grill cover with the pot still on the grate. Smoke for 5 minutes or until the rice is cooked through.

8. Serve the Arroz Caldo hot in bowls. Garnish with green onion, lemon slices, crispy fried garlic, and egg slices, as you prefer.

PORK BELLY TOCINO BREAKFAST BURRITO

YIELD: 4 burritos — PREP: 45 minutes — MARINATING: 1 to 24 hours — COOK: 1 hour

Pork belly is really just another name for the best bacon you'll ever eat. A lot of Pitmasters lean into a sweet, maple syrup–based glaze, but I go in a different direction with this breakfast meal-in-one. I wanted to brighten the flavors a little bit and add a sour bite, so I landed on the unique sweet-sour vibe of cane vinegar and the tart sweetness of pineapple juice. Trust me, it's an amazing way to start any morning.

For the Marinade

½ cup (115 g) packed light brown sugar

1 tablespoon (14 g) kosher salt

1 tablespoon (8 g) coarse ground black pepper

1 tablespoon (14 g) garlic paste

1 tablespoon (15 ml) soy sauce

2 tablespoons (28 ml) cane vinegar

½ cup (120 ml) pineapple juice

Natural red food color (optional)

1½ pounds (680 g) pork belly

For the Burrito

1 package (16 ounces, or 455 g) hash browns

8 large eggs

Taco seasoning (or preferred spice blend) to taste

4 large flour tortillas

1 package (16 ounces, or 455 g) shredded cheese

Hot sauce to taste

1. In a large bowl, combine the marinade ingredients and mix well. Slice the pork belly into 2- to 3-inch (5 to 7.5 cm) strips and toss them in the marinade. Cover and refrigerate for at least 1 hour and preferably overnight (or use a chamber vacuum sealer with an instant marinate function to marinate in a couple of minutes).

2. Preheat a griddle over medium-high heat and cook the hash browns next to the eggs. Dust the eggs with taco seasoning (or whatever spice blend you prefer) and scramble them. Remove and set aside.

3. Cook the pork belly on the griddle, turning often. Cook for 5 to 10 minutes or until cooked through and slightly blackened.

4. Lay a tortilla flat. Spread a wide line of hash browns across the center. Top with a line of the eggs, a mound of the pork belly, and a layer of the cheese. Sprinkle with hot sauce.

5. Pull up one edge of the burrito while folding in the sides and rolling it toward the opposite edge. Roll it tightly and then grill the lip of the burrito closed, leaving it on the grill for about 2 minutes or until the bottom of the burrito is deep brown. Repeat with the remaining tortillas.

6. Slice a burrito in half across its width, spread with more hot sauce as desired, and dig in!

BISTEK TAGALOG

YIELD: 4 to 6 servings — PREP: 15 minutes — MARINATING: 30 to 60 minutes — COOK: 40 minutes

I'm a Bay Area guy now, but my roots on my dad's side run back to the island of Luzon's Tagalog region. This soul-satisfying dish is a nod to that heritage and a tasty gift from a part of my culture to yours. Bistek is Spanish for "beefsteak," and I put my own spin on the traditional version because, hey, there's always room for more flavor. I use lemon in mine, but if you can get them locally, substitute calamansi for the lemon. Calamansi is a cross between a lemon and a lime that is only grown in the Philippines.

For the Marinade

1 large yellow onion, peeled and sliced

1 head garlic, peeled and minced

1 tablespoon (8 g) coarse ground black pepper

½ cup (120 ml) freshly squeezed lemon juice

½ cup (120 ml) soy sauce

2 pounds (910 g) thinly sliced beef short ribs (also known as Korean short ribs)

1 to 2 tablespoons (15 to 28 ml) Worcestershire sauce (I use Bear & Burton's Fireshire.)

1 cup (225 ml) water

Salt to taste

2 cups (316 g) long-grain white rice, cooked

1 lemon, halved

1. Preheat the grill to medium-high (about 350°F, or 180°C).

2. In a large bowl, combine the onions (reserving a few slices), garlic, pepper, lemon juice, and soy sauce for the marinade. Mix together well. Massage the marinade into the short ribs and then nestle the beef in the marinade. Cover and refrigerate for at least 30 minutes and up to 1 hour.

3. Remove the meat from the marinade and drain any excess, reserving the marinade. Grill the short ribs 1 to 2 minutes on each side, just enough to get a quick sear and char. Set aside.

4. Preheat a large pan or cast-iron skillet over medium-high heat.

5. Transfer the onions and garlic from the marinade to the skillet. Add the Fireshire. Cook until soft and the onions are turning translucent. Add the reserved marinade and bring to a boil.

6. Add the short ribs, water, and salt. Cover, reduce the heat to low, and simmer for 40 minutes. Stir after 20 minutes.

7. Remove the pan from the heat. Add in the reserved onion slices, cover, and let steam for 5 to 10 minutes. Serve over white rice spritzed with freshly squeezed lemon. Enjoy!

BISTEK BEEF SKEWERS

YIELD: 4 servings — PREP: 20 minutes — MARINATING: 1 hour — COOK: 10 to 15 minutes

These skewers are easy and quick to make, the perfect thing for a spur-of-the-moment backyard get-together. They fit anywhere in a meal; they can be entrée, a side dish, an appetizer, or a snack. You can also mix them up and go a little more traditional by alternating the skewered meat with cherry tomatoes, pineapple chunks, mushrooms, or whatever your favorite veggie might be. No matter what, skewers are the perfect way to get the best out of tri-tip steak. The cut naturally holds up well when it's grilled in small pieces, and tri-tip has a rich beef flavor that can go toe to toe with much more expensive cuts.

1½ pounds (680 g) tri-tip steak (or substitute your favorite cut)

For the Marinade

1 large white onion, peeled and sliced

1 head garlic, peeled and minced

1 to 2 tablespoons (15 to 28 ml) Worcestershire sauce (I use Bear & Burton's Fireshire.)

Salt to taste

1 tablespoon (8 g) coarse ground black pepper

2 large lemons, halved

1 cup (235 ml) water

½ cup (120 ml) white vinegar

1. Slice the steak lengthwise into strips approximately 1-inch (2.5 cm) thick. Cut each strip into medallions. Transfer to a large bowl.

2. Add the onion and garlic to the bowl. Pour in the Fireshire and season with the salt and pepper. Spritz with lemon juice from the lemon halves and toss the squeezed halves into the bowl. Add the water and vinegar.

3. Toss the meat in the marinade until all the ingredients are well combined and the beef is completely coated. Cover the bowl with plastic wrap and refrigerate for 1 hour.

4. Preheat the grill over medium-high heat, about 350°F (180°C). Skewer the meat and grill to your desired doneness, turning frequently. (Grill for about 10 minutes for medium-rare and about 15 for medium-well.)

FILIPINO BBQ PORK SKEWERS

YIELD: 4 servings — PREP: 1 hour — MARINATING: 3 to 24 hours — COOK: 20 minutes

Filipinos love them some lemon soda. It's naturally refreshing and goes with Filipino food like jelly goes with peanut butter. So it's only natural that I'd give a nod to that love in the zesty, fizzy marinade I make for my Filipino-style pork skewers. I'm not going to judge you if you add veggies to your skewers, but I look at that as space that could have gone to spicy, sweet, piquant pork. And what are you gaining? A cherry tomato. Really? Dude, c'mon. Roll in Filipino style and crowd those skewers with this delectable meat.

1 pork shoulder (4 pounds, or 1.8 kg)

For both the Marinade and the Basting Sauce

1½ cups (355 ml) soy sauce

1 cup (235 ml) lemon juice

1½ cups (360 g) spicy banana ketchup

½ cup (115 g) packed light brown sugar

¼ cup (36 g) garlic powder

2 teaspoons freshly ground black pepper

¼ cup (72 g) salt

1½ cups (355 ml) lemon or lime soda

1. Cut the pork into roughly 2-inch (5 cm) chunks. In a large bowl, combine all the marinade and basting sauce ingredients except for the soda and mix well. Divide into two equal portions and set aside half the mixture for basting. Stir the soda into the marinade portion.

2. Transfer the pork to a large bowl and pour the marinade over the pork. Toss until well coated. Cover and refrigerate for at least 3 hours and preferably overnight.

3. Prepare your grill with your favorite briquettes to high heat or about 400°F (200°C). Slide the pork onto the skewers.

4. Grill the skewers for 3 to 5 minutes per side or until the meat is nicely charred and cooked through (the internal temperature for pork should always reach at least 145°F [63°C]). Flip the skewers several times during grilling, brushing with the basting sauce after every flip.

5. Remove and let rest for 3 to 5 minutes or until the meat is cooled enough to handle. Serve and enjoy!

BBQ ADOBO SPARERIBS

YIELD: 6 servings — PREP: 45 minutes — MARINATING: 1 hour — COOK: 3½ hours

Adobo is a prep style that boasts some of the best flavors the Philippines has to offer. This BBQ favorite is always welcome at the table thanks to a vinegar-fueled balance of sweet and sour and a magic blend of spices that brings out the absolute best in any protein. Adobo is a great way to prepare any pork, but it's particularly dope for spareribs because the bones keep the meat juicy and add flavor that takes the adobo spice blend to the next level. I keep my version pretty basic because I wanted the classic flavors to dominate. The people I feed can't get enough.

1 rack whole spareribs (1½ to 2 pounds, or 680 to 910 g)

For the Marinade

1 cup (235 ml) low-sodium soy sauce

1 cup (235 ml) coconut vinegar (or substitute white vinegar)

2 tablespoons (28 g) garlic paste

1 tablespoon (8 g) freshly ground black pepper (or substitute whole peppercorns [5 g], crushed)

½ white onion, peeled and sliced

3 to 4 bay leaves

3 tablespoons (36 g) BBQ rub of choice

1 cup (225 g) packed light brown sugar

For Serving

2 green onions, chopped (optional)

Crispy fried garlic (optional)

(CONTINUED)

1. Prep the ribs by trimming the flap off the back and peeling the membrane off (if you don't want to tackle that, have the butcher prepare the ribs for you).

2. In a small bowl, combine the soy sauce, vinegar, garlic, and pepper and stir them until completely mixed. Transfer the ribs into a shallow roasting pan. Pour the marinade over the ribs and add the onions and bay leaves. Cover and marinate in the fridge for at least 1 hour, turning the ribs once.

3. Prepare the smoker with the wood of your choice to medium-high heat, 275°F to 300°F (140°C to 150°C). Remove the ribs from the roasting pan, reserving the marinade. Pat dry and coat both sides of the ribs with the rub. You'll smoke the ribs for a total of 3 hours.

4. Transfer the marinade to a large pot over medium heat. Bring to a boil and then reduce to a simmer. Simmer for 10 to 15 minutes or until the liquid reduces slightly and thickens.

5. Remove the onions and bay leaves from the sauce. Stir in the brown sugar and continue to simmer until the adobo glaze is thick enough to coat the back of a large spoon.

6. After the ribs have been smoking for 2½ hours, slather the ribs with the adobo glaze on both sides. Smoke for another 30 minutes or until the internal temperature reaches 195°F to 200°F (91°C to 93°C). Take the ribs out of the smoker and let them rest for 15 minutes.

7. Slice the ribs and drizzle with the rest of the adobo glaze. Sprinkle with green onions and crispy fried garlic, if desired, before serving.

ADOBO BRISKET BURNT ENDS
WITH CRAB FRIED RICE

YIELD: 4 to 6 servings — PREP: 45 minutes — MARINATING: 2 to 24 hours — COOK: 8 to 10 hours

When it comes to BBQ, few cuts can match a brisket for pure potential. This is a flavor-packed piece of meat from the chest of the cow, well marbled with delicious fat that keeps the meat juicy during long, low-and-slow smoking. The two parts of the brisket are the flat and the point. The flat is huge and the point is about one-fifth the size, making it an easier piece of meat for backyard pit jockeys to handle. You can find the cuts prepackaged, but you usually guarantee quality by getting your brisket from a butcher. They can also trim the fat cap off the cut, which is part of prepping it for smoking.

For the Marinade

- 2 cups (475 ml) low-sodium soy sauce
- 1 cup (235 ml) calamansi juice (or substitute lemon juice)
- 6 cloves garlic, peeled
- 1 tablespoon (5 g) black peppercorns
- 1 tablespoon (15 g) dark brown sugar
- 2 tablespoons (3 g) annatto powder (optional)
- 4 bay leaves

- 1 brisket (2 pounds, or 910 g)

For the Rub

- 2 tablespoons (28 g) kosher salt
- 2 tablespoons (16 g) coarse ground black pepper
- 1 tablespoon (7 g) smoked paprika
- 1 tablespoon (9 g) garlic powder
- 1 tablespoon (7 g) onion powder
- 1 tablespoon (3 g) dried oregano
- 1 tablespoon (15 g) light brown sugar
- 1 teaspoon annatto powder (optional)

- ½ cup (120 ml) Worcestershire sauce (I use Bear & Burton's Fireshire.)

For the Sauce

- 2 tablespoons (16 g) cornstarch
- ½ cup (120 ml) water
- 1 cup (225 g) packed light brown sugar
- 1 cup (235 ml) cane vinegar
- 2–3 tablespoons (40–60 g) honey

(CONTINUED)

For the Crab Fried Rice

1 tablespoon (15 ml) olive oil

10 cloves garlic, peeled and minced

4–6 cups (744 g–1.1 kg) day-old cooked rice

2 tablespoons (28 ml) low-sodium soy sauce

1 tablespoon (15 ml) fish sauce

2 teaspoons white pepper

1 cup (or 135 g) crabmeat

4 large eggs

2 tablespoons (12 g) chopped green onions

For Serving

2 tablespoons (12 g) crispy fried garlic (optional)

2 tablespoons (12 g) chopped scallions (optional)

1. In a large plastic pan with a lid, combine all the marinade ingredients. Mix thoroughly. Nestle the brisket in the marinade, cover, and refrigerate for at least 2 hours and preferably overnight (or even longer).

2. Remove the brisket from the marinade and pat dry (leave the marinade in the pan and set aside in the fridge). Combine the rub ingredients in a shaker and mix well. Smear the brisket all over with the Worcestershire sauce and then coat liberally with the rub.

3. Prepare the smoker with charcoal and oak to about 250°F (120°C). Smoke the brisket for 4 to 6 hours or until the internal temperature reaches 170°F (77°C). Remove and let rest for 15 minutes.

4. Cut the brisket into roughly 2-inch (5 cm) cubes. Transfer the cubes and the reserved marinade to a pan that will fit in the smoker, cover, and place the pan in the smoker. Smoke for another 3 to 4 hours or until the brisket is probe tender and the internal temperature reaches 203°F (95°C).

5. Mix the cornstarch and water together to form a slurry. In a large pot, pour in the remaining marinade from the cubes and combine with the brown sugar, vinegar, and honey for the sauce. Simmer over medium heat for 15 to 20 minutes or until the sauce is reduced by half. Remove the bay leaves from the sauce. Stir in the cornstarch slurry to thicken and bind.

6. While the sauce is reducing, make the Crab Fried Rice. In a cast-iron skillet over medium heat, heat the oil and add the garlic. Cook for 1 to 2 minutes, just until the garlic starts to brown. Add the rice, toss, and drizzle with the soy sauce. Stir and then add the remaining ingredients. Keep stirring until the eggs are completely cooked.

7. Transfer the brisket cubes to a large bowl, drizzle with the sauce, and toss to coat. Serve the burnt ends over a mound of the Crab Fried Rice, drizzled with more sauce as desired. Garnish with the crispy fried garlic and scallions, if using.

ADOBO BBQ CHICKEN

YIELD: 2 to 4 servings — PREP: 1 hour — MARINATING: 8 to 12 hours — COOK: 1 hour

If you've never spatchcocked a chicken, you haven't taken full advantage of the bird. Spatchcocking is essentially deboning most of the chicken and breaking the bones that remain so that the chicken lays flat. It's a handy technique for grilling or smoking because it can speed up the cooking process and creates a lot more surface area to hold a rub or a sauce (or both!). That's important when you're aiming for the big flavor profile of adobo, with the tang of vinegar playing off the caramel sweetness of brown sugar and honey. Spatchcocking also ensures a nice surface crust from the adobo glaze, which is sure to keep your people happy.

1 whole chicken (1½ pounds, or 680 g)

For the Marinade and Adobo Glaze

1 cup (235 ml) soy sauce

1 cup (235 ml) white vinegar

1 cup (235 ml) water

½ white onion, peeled and sliced

1 head garlic, peeled and chopped

1 jalapeño, sliced

5 bay leaves

1 cup (225 g) packed dark brown sugar

1 tablespoon (20 g) honey

1. Spatchcock the chicken by cutting along each side of the back with kitchen shears. Remove the spine of the chicken, turn it over, and use a heavy weight to press down and crack the breast. (Or, if you're in a hurry to get to the smoking, have a butcher spatchcock the chicken for you.)

2. In a large 4-quart (3.4 L) pot, combine the soy sauce, vinegar, water, onion, garlic, jalapeño, and bay leaves. Add the chicken to the pot, nestling it in the marinade. Cover and refrigerate overnight.

3. Remove the chicken and reserve the marinade. Prepare your smoker with your favorite wood to a temperature of 250°F to 275°F (120°C to 140°C). Transfer the chicken to the smoker and close the lid.

4. While the chicken is smoking, bring the marinade to a slow boil over low heat. Strain the marinade and return the liquid to the pot. Add the brown sugar and honey. Lower the heat to a simmer and reduce the sauce by half.

5. Smoke the chicken for 30 to 35 minutes or until the internal temperature reaches 165°F (74°C) in the thickest part of the breast. Baste the chicken all over with the adobo glaze and continue smoking until the internal temperature reaches 170°F (77°C). The outside of the chicken will blacken thanks to the sugar in the glaze. Just be careful that it doesn't burn.

6. Remove the chicken and let it rest for 15 minutes. Baste it one last time with the remaining glaze, slice it up, and serve it to hungry friends and family.

DYNAMITE LUMPIA

YIELD: 4 servings — PREP: 30 minutes — COOK: 10 minutes

This is my take on one of the most popular street foods in the Philippines. Called dinamita, *it's simple and satisfying as much for its mix of textures as for its bang of flavor. The fried, crispy shell hides melty cheese and crumbles of perfectly cooked bacon. There's one important note, though: You shouldn't substitute egg roll wrappers for actual lumpia wrappers. Lumpia wrappers are thinner and less gummy, so they make the perfect crunch for the teeth when fried up—not so much with egg roll wrappers. Ultimately, these are so simple to make, I'm not sure why you wouldn't put them into a weekly rotation.*

1 package (8 ounces, or 225 g) cream cheese

1 package (16 ounces, or 455 g) Mexican-style shredded cheese blend

½ cup (40 g) crumbled cooked bacon

¼ cup (48 g) BBQ rub of choice

8–10 jalapeños

1 large egg

1 tablespoon (15 ml) water

8–10 lumpia wrappers

2 cups (475 ml) peanut oil

1. In a large bowl, use a fork to mash together the cream cheese, shredded cheese, bacon, and BBQ rub until thoroughly mixed.

2. Halve the jalapeños lengthwise and remove the seeds and veins. Fill each half with the cheese mixture. Press the halves together to re-form the whole jalapeños. In a small bowl, combine the egg and water and whisk to a uniform texture.

3. Fold down one corner of a lumpia wrapper and center a jalapeño on the fold, with the tip pointed to the center of the wrapper. Fold the opposite corner over the tip of the pepper and then roll it up from one of the remaining corners. Brush egg wash on the remaining corner and fold it over to close the roll. Repeat with the remaining jalapeños and wrappers.

4. In a large pot or fryer, heat the peanut oil to 350°F (180°C). Fry the lumpias about 2 minutes on each side or until golden brown, turning midway through frying. Only fry a few at a time; crowding the oil lowers the frying temperature and makes for greasy lumpias.

5. When the fried lumpias are cool enough to be handled, serve with the condiment of your choice. I like spicy vinegar with mine.

NUTELLA TURON LUMPIA

YIELD: 4 to 6 servings — PREP: 15 minutes — COOK: 40 minutes

Lumpias are basically the Filipino version of egg rolls, but more adaptable. They can be made with meat, vegetables, or like in this recipe, as the ultimate meal-ending dessert. The contrast of crunchy shell wrapped around the silky softness of chocolate-drenched bananas makes these sugary treasures incredibly satisfying. After the fire, it's always good to have something sweet and creamy. So here you go.

1 cup (200 g) granulated sugar

5 tablespoons (70 g) salted butter

½ cup plus 1 tablespoon (135 ml) heavy cream

Pinch sea salt, plus more for dusting

4–5 large Saba bananas (or substitute 3 traditional bananas, see note on page 59)

10–12 lumpia wrappers

⅓ cup (99 g) chocolate hazelnut spread (I use Nutella.)

2 cups (475 ml) peanut oil

1. Heat a large pan over medium heat. Add the granulated sugar and stir continuously until the sugar is completely melted and turning from light to dark brown. Pay very close attention because the sugar can burn in a heartbeat. That said, the longer you cook it, the darker the caramel and the richer the flavor.

2. When the sugar is the desired color, turn off the heat and add the butter, continuing to stir. Once the butter is melted and incorporated, slowly pour in the heavy cream (it will bubble up, but then settle). Keep stirring until the consistency is even. Sprinkle in the salt.

3. Peel the bananas and trim the ends. Slice each banana in half, lengthwise, and then slice each half lengthwise again. (Each quarter should wind up about 4 inches [10 cm] long.)

4. Spread out one lumpia wrapper and smear it with about 1 tablespoon (19 g) chocolate hazelnut spread. Center a banana quarter on it. Fold one corner of the wrapper over the banana. Fold both ends in over the ends of the banana and then roll up the lumpia the rest of the way. Seal the lip of the final corner with a brush of water and press firmly to secure the roll. Repeat with the rest of the wrappers.

5. In a deep skillet or fryer, heat the peanut oil to 350°F (180°C). Fry two lumpias at a time; crowding the oil lowers the frying temperature and makes for greasy lumpias. Flip each lumpia halfway through and fry them until they are dark golden brown all around.

6. Let the lumpias cool for about 5 minutes or until cool enough to handle, then drizzle with the caramel, sprinkle with more sea salt, and enjoy!

The Better Banana

Although they're not available everywhere, Saba bananas are native to the Philippines and a rich flavor alternative to regular bananas. They are shorter and fatter, with a thicker skin and a higher starch content, making the texture a little like plantains (Sabas are sometimes sold as "sweet plantain"). But they have a deep, complex taste and are sweeter than plantains or most store-bought bananas. Be careful: Once you discover the flavor of a Saba, average supermarket bananas will never seem good enough again!

LUMPIA WITH SAWSAWAN

YIELD: 8 to 10 lumpias — PREP: 15 minutes — COOK: 10 minutes

Sawsawan—the word actually translates to "dipping sauce"—is a classic Filipino dipping sauce. Make this recipe, and you'll discover why it's so beloved. This is just one more example of Filipino cooking's mastery in playing savory against sour or tangy. It's endlessly interesting on the tongue. The really intriguing thing about that balance is that it ensures something like sawsawan goes with just about anything you can imagine—from cut vegetables to smoked meat to steamed seafood. (I haven't ever topped ice cream with it, but . . . it's worth a try!) In this case, the sauce provides a brilliant, bright counterweight to a rich, filling bite of beef-packed lumpia. I guarantee, neither of these will disappoint.

For the Sawsawan Sauce

1 head garlic, peeled and chopped

1 large shallot, peeled and chopped

1 red chili, sliced

1 large jalapeño, sliced

1 teaspoon salt

1 teaspoon freshly ground black pepper

1 tablespoon (15 g) light brown sugar

2 tablespoons (28 ml) fish sauce

2 tablespoons (28 ml) water

1 cup (235 ml) cane vinegar

For the Filling

1 package (14 ounces, or 395 g) Ibérico pork and Wagyu beef blend (such as the Ground Ibérico-Wagyu Blend by Campo Grande)

2 tablespoons (20 g) minced garlic

2 tablespoons (20 g) minced shallot

½ cup (1 ounce, or 50 g) grated carrot

1 teaspoon garlic powder

1 teaspoon salt

1 teaspoon coarse ground black pepper

1 teaspoon ground cayenne pepper

For the Lumpias

8 to 10 lumpia wrappers

2 cups (475 ml) peanut oil

(CONTINUED)

1. Combine all the ingredients for the sauce in a Mason jar and shake until emulsified.

2. In a large cast-iron skillet over medium heat, brown the meat blend. Transfer it to a large bowl. Bump the heat up to high and cook the remaining filling ingredients in the same skillet. When the vegetables are softened, about 8 minutes, add the meat back into the skillet and mix thoroughly. Remove from the heat.

3. Lay a lumpia wrapper flat. Scoop a heaping spoonful of filling in the center and fold over one corner to the center. Begin rolling from the fold and tuck in the two opposite corners as you fold. Wet the final corner and roll the lumpia tightly closed. Repeat with the rest of the filling and wrappers.

4. In a deep cast-iron skillet or fryer, heat the oil to 350°F (180°C). Fry two lumpias at a time; crowding the oil lowers the frying temperature and makes for greasy lumpias. Flip each lumpia halfway through frying. Fry them until they are golden brown all around.

5. Let the lumpias cool for about 5 minutes or until they are cool enough to handle. Serve with the sawsawan and enjoy!

BUFFALO CHICKEN LUMPIA

YIELD: 8 to 10 lumpias — PREP: 1 hour — MARINATING: 1 hour — COOK: 1½ hours

Mash together an American classic and a Filipino staple and what do you get? BBQ perfection that will rock the house. This is as simple as simple can be and is an amazing weeknight go-to that will create a real special-occasion feel to a basic dinner. It's also a tremendous additional dish for a much bigger spread or as one element of a party food spread. No matter what, this lumpia stands out for its giant flavors in a small, portable package. It's easy as can be to make, satisfyingly crispy, and purely delicious.

2 chicken breasts (10 ounces, or 285 g each)

¼ cup (60 ml) buffalo wing sauce, divided, plus more for serving

1 package (4 ounces, or 115 g) blue cheese crumbles

8–10 lumpia wrappers

2 cups (475 ml) peanut oil

Ranch dressing

1. In a large bowl, coat the chicken breasts all over with 2 tablespoons (28 ml) of the buffalo wing sauce. Refrigerate and marinate for 1 hour.

2. Prepare the smoker with your favorite wood, heated to about 325°F (190°C). Smoke the breasts for about 1 hour or until the internal temperature reaches 165°F (74°C). Remove and let rest for 20 to 30 minutes.

3. Shred and roughly chop the chicken. Transfer to a large bowl and top with the blue cheese crumbles and remaining buffalo wing sauce. Mix well.

4. Lay a lumpia wrapper flat. Scoop a heaping spoonful of the chicken mixture in a line from one corner to the other. Fold over a third corner to the center. Begin rolling from the folded corner, slightly tucking in the two ends of the chicken mix line as you roll. Wet the final corner and roll the lumpia tightly closed. Repeat with the rest of the chicken mixture.

5. In a deep cast-iron skillet or fryer, heat the oil to 350°F (180°C). Fry two lumpias at a time; crowding the oil lowers the frying temperature and makes for greasy lumpias. Fry for about 1 minute each side, flipping halfway through. Fry them until they are golden brown all around.

6. Drizzle the lumpias with more buffalo wing sauce as desired and serve with your favorite ranch dressing.

CAJUN FIRE AND SMOKE

Cajun cooking is a combination of rustic French and southern cuisines. It leans more country because the style comes right out of the bayou. It's all about spicy, not just hot. Cajun spice blends create flavor explosions that leave you sorting out everything that's happening on your tongue.

The style is super adaptable. My mother, a Cajun through and through, was into fusion long before I was. She dominated the kitchen. She was bold and assertive, just like Cajun cooking. I watched her cook traditional Filipino dishes with a Cajun spin, creating food that was completely original and strangely familiar all at the same time. She loved Hungarian cooking, and would put a Cajun spice spin on classic Hungarian dishes to create intensely delicious meals. She

was always playing around with the Cajun basics. We loved everything that came out of her kitchen.

Cajun cooking is all about the mix of spices. The traditional flavors include healthy amounts of paprika, cayenne, thyme, and gumbo filé, along with more than a little butter. Although Cajun style focuses on foods that could be harvested in the bayou, like shrimp and crawfish, the spices translate to any protein you might put on a grill or in a smoker.

My mom's kitchen is where I got my love of cast-iron cookware. Cajun cooks like cast-iron because it's durable; they can pop a skillet full of etouffee right into the oven. Cast iron heats evenly and if seasoned properly, is a breeze to clean. I often cook side dishes or sauces right on the grill in a cast-iron skillet or pot.

Cajuns have a saying that applies to both their cooking and how they live: *Laissez les bons temps rouler.* It translates to "Let the good times roll." I hope the recipes in this chapter inspire you to BBQ your own good times.

CAJUN HONEY BUTTER SHRIMP

YIELD: 4 servings — PREP: 20 minutes — COOK: 15 minutes

Shrimp, like chicken, is a flavor-delivery vehicle. These shellfish are canvases you can paint on with spices. Lots of cooks like to add healthy doses of garlic to their honey butter shrimp, while others swear by Old Bay Seasoning. Me? I prefer to develop my own spice blends, which I did for the honey butter in this recipe. Replacing the traditional water in the egg wash with pale ale is a small tweak that pays off in a surprisingly big way. Don't be afraid to experiment with your own adjustments and your favorite beer. The shrimp won't mind!

For the Egg Wash

¼ cup (60 ml) pale beer (I use Firestone Walker 805 California Blonde Ale.)

3 large eggs, beaten

For the Dredge

1 cup (50 g) panko breadcrumbs

1 cup (128 g) cornstarch

2 tablespoons (24 g) spicy BBQ rub (I use Blazing Star Reaper Rub and Seasoning.)

For the Shrimp

2 pounds (910 g) jumbo shrimp, peeled and deveined

2 cups (475 ml) peanut oil

For the Cajun Honey Butter

6 tablespoons (85 g) unsalted butter, room temperature

2 teaspoons garlic powder

2 teaspoons Italian seasoning

2 teaspoons smoked paprika

1 teaspoon ground cayenne pepper

2 teaspoons onion powder

1 teaspoon coarse ground black pepper

½ teaspoon salt

½ teaspoon crushed red pepper flakes

3 tablespoons (60 g) honey

1. In a wide, shallow bowl, combine the beer and eggs. Whisk until the consistency is uniform. In a separate wide, shallow bowl, whisk together the dredge ingredients.

2. Thoroughly coat each shrimp in the egg wash. Press the shrimp into the dredge, breading each shrimp all around.

3. In a deep cast-iron skillet or pot, heat about ½ inch (1.3 cm) of peanut oil to 350°F (180°C). Begin frying the shrimp in batches; don't crowd them or you risk lowering the oil temperature. Once they are deep golden brown, transfer the shrimp to a platter lined with paper towels.

4. While the shrimp fries, make the Cajun Honey Butter. In a small cast-iron saucepot over medium-low heat, melt the butter. Add the remaining ingredients and stir. Simmer until the mixture has thickened enough to coat the back of a spoon.

5. Drizzle the fried shrimp with the Cajun Honey Butter and serve.

CAJUN HONEY BUTTER SALMON

YIELD: 6 to 8 servings — PREP: 10 minutes — COOK: 45 to 60 minutes

The butter in this recipe elevates anything it touches, but you'll do the dish proud by using the best salmon you can find. Whether you're cooking BBQ or steaming the fish, buy fresh because quality salmon is key. I work mostly with fillets, which are cut along the length of the fish and rarely have bones (as opposed to the steaks cut across the fish's body, which often involve picking out small bones). Regardless, look for wild salmon with a dark pink, almost red color. There really shouldn't be any smell to fresh salmon, and the flesh should be firm and just slightly moist. Although reputable stores often sell packaged cuts that are perfectly fine, you'll get the best, freshest salmon at a seafood store. Planning a big cookout? You can buy a whole salmon and have fishmonger cut it for you.

2 salmon fillets (2½ pounds, or 1.1 kg)

For the Cajun Butter

6 tablespoons (85 g) unsalted butter, room temperature

2 teaspoons garlic powder

2 teaspoons Italian seasoning

2 teaspoons smoked paprika

1 teaspoon ground cayenne pepper

2 teaspoons onion powder

1 teaspoon coarse ground black pepper

½ teaspoon salt

½ teaspoon crushed red pepper flakes

3 tablespoons (60 g) honey

3 tablespoons (9 g) chopped fresh chives

1. Soak two cedar planks in water for 1 hour. In a large bowl, combine all the ingredients for the Cajun Butter, except for the honey. Mix well. (If the butter is not completely softened, put it in an oven or smoker for 1 minute or until soft.)

2. Prepare a smoker with your favorite wood, heated to about 300°F (150°C).

3. Lay each salmon fillet on a plank and pat dry. Coat liberally with the Cajun Butter, reserving 2 to 3 tablespoons (28 to 45 ml).

4. Transfer the planks to the smoker and smoke the salmon for about 45 minutes or to your preferred doneness. I cook mine to an internal temperature of 130°F (54°C), but many people prefer, and the FDA recommends, an internal temperature of 145°F (63°C).

5. In a small cast-iron saucepot over medium heat, warm the honey. Remove the salmon and drizzle with the reserved Cajun Butter and the warmed honey. Sprinkle with the chives and enjoy.

CAJUN HONEY BUTTER LOBSTER

YIELD: 4 servings — PREP: 10 minutes — COOK: 30 minutes

This is an upgrade from the traditional Cajun crawdad dishes. Lobster brings an intense, rich sweetness that is just perfect for smoking and a great counterpoint to the slap-you-in-the-face Cajun spices and hot honey. Lobster isn't cheap, so it's smart to check the details before you buy. A gray shade means that the tail was preserved quickly, after the lobster was dead, using chemicals—that's never a good sign. You want a hard, thick shell, and there shouldn't be much of an odor. If the tails smell fishy or sour like buttermilk, shop somewhere else.

6 tablespoons (85 g) unsalted butter, room temperature

8 cloves garlic, peeled and minced

3 tablespoons (30 g) no-salt Cajun seasoning

2–3 tablespoons (40–60 g) of chili-infused hot honey (I use Mike's Hot Honey.)

2 large lobster tails (10–12 ounces, or 280–340 g each)

2 tablespoons (6 g) chopped fresh chives

1. Prepare the smoker with your wood of choice, heated to about 350°F (180°C).

2. In a small bowl, combine the butter, garlic, seasoning, and hot honey. Mash them together until they are completely combined and form a thick paste.

3. Rinse the lobster tails and use shears to cut down the center of the shells and the membrane underneath. Spread the shell and scoop the hot honey butter all over the flesh. Insert a probe from a wireless meat thermometer into each lobster tail.

4. Smoke for about 20 minutes or until the internal temperature reaches 135°F (57°C). Remove the lobster and let rest for about 5 minutes.

5. Remove the shells and slice the lobster meat into 2-inch (5 cm) chunks. Drizzle with the melted butter drippings, sprinkle with chives, and serve.

SMOKED CAJUN JAMBALAYA

YIELD: 4 to 6 servings — **PREP: 20 minutes** — **COOK: 1 hour**

You couldn't get more Cajun than my mom's kitchen or the classic jambalaya she made on special occasions. This all-in-one stew is the heart of culinary Louisiana and uses all the great ingredients you'll find in the bayou or any Cajun kitchen. My mom put her own spin on the dish, and now, so have I. Jambalaya is a symphony of flavors, and I let the spice section play loudly. It's not just heat. I worked to balance the fire with a little smoke and some earthy notes. Go ahead and double up the recipe if you want; it keeps well.

2 large boneless chicken breasts (8–10 ounces, or 225–280 g each)

2 tablespoons (24 g) spice-and-herb seasoning (I use Tony Chachere's Spice N' Herbs Creole Seasoning.)

1 tablespoon (15 ml) olive oil

4 tablespoons (55 g) unsalted butter, divided

½ pound (455 g) peeled 51/60 shrimp

½ cup (120 ml) seafood marinade (I use Tony Chachere's Creole-Style Seafood Pourable Marinade.)

12 ounces (340 g) andouille sausage

1 stalk celery, diced

1 large green bell pepper, seeded and chopped

1 teaspoon smoked paprika

1 teaspoon dried oregano

1 teaspoon dried thyme

1 teaspoon garlic powder

1 teaspoon onion powder

1 teaspoon freshly ground black pepper

2 tablespoons (20 g) salt-free seasoning blend (I use Tony Chachere's No Salt Seasoning.)

1 can (14½ ounces, or 410 g) fire-roasted diced tomatoes

1 cup (210 g) long grain white rice

1½ cups (355 ml) chicken broth

2 green onions, sliced (for garnish)

(CONTINUED)

1. Season the chicken breasts with the spice-and-herb seasoning blend.

2. Preheat a cast-iron pan over medium-high heat. When the pan is hot, drizzle in the olive oil and lay a chicken breast into the pan. Sear on each side for 3 to 5 minutes until each side is crusted. Move the chicken to a plate. Repeat with the second chicken breast.

3. Center 1 tablespoon (14 g) of butter on a large aluminum foil square, sit a chicken breast on top, and top it with another 1 tablespoon (14 g) of butter. Wrap tightly and set aside. Repeat with the second chicken breast.

4. In a small bowl, combine the shrimp and the seafood marinade. Mix well. Cover and refrigerate for 15 minutes or use a chamber vacuum sealer set to the instant marinate option.

5. In the pan you used for the chicken, cook the shrimp over medium heat for about 1 minute on each side. Transfer to a plate and set aside. Brown the sausage in the same pan, cooking it for 5 to 10 minutes or until nicely crusted. Transfer to a plate and set aside.

6. Combine the celery and bell pepper with the spices in the same pan. Return the sausage and shrimp to the pan and stir in the tomatoes, rice, and chicken broth. Stir thoroughly until completely combined. Continue heating over medium heat.

7. While the pan comes to a simmer, prepare a smoker with applewood, heated to about 350°F (180°C). Place the pan into smoker, along with both of the foil-wrapped chicken breasts, and smoke for 15 to 25 minutes. Stir the pan mixture every 5 minutes to ensure the top doesn't dry out. Regularly check the internal temperature of the chicken breasts. Remove them from the smoker when they reach an internal temperature of 165°F (74°C).

8. When the jambalaya and chicken are both cooked completely, remove and let rest for about 5 minutes. Slice the chicken and place on top of the jambalaya. Sprinkle the green onions over top and serve hot.

CAJUN LOCO MOCO

YIELD: 4 servings — PREP: 30 minutes — COOK: 90 minutes

Haven't ever heard of loco moco? *Where have you been? This traditional island breakfast boasts a unique blend of flavors and textures. It was invented in Hawaii, but it's become a favorite far from the islands because it's such an interesting and delicious way to start the day. That said, it's as friendly for dinner as it is for breakfast because it combines something from the sea and something from the pasture. I wanted my version to kick everything up a gear. That meant going a little bit Louisiana on the spice blend and using a heavy hand with the garlic. It's ten kinds of satisfying right here. Maybe you should make it tonight and find out for yourself.*

¼ cup (60 ml) vegetable oil

¼ cup (31 g) all-purpose flour

1 stalk celery, chopped

1 green bell pepper, seeded and chopped

4 jalapeños, chopped

½ large onion, peeled and chopped

1 head garlic, peeled and minced

2 cups (475 ml) seafood stock

1–2 tablespoons (8–16 g) cornstarch, for a slurry (optional)

2 pounds (910 g) medium shrimp, shelled and deveined

2 tablespoons (24 g) Cajun seasoning, divided

½ teaspoon celery seed

1 tablespoon (7 g) smoked paprika

Salt to taste

4 green onions, sliced

4 premade hamburger patties (4 ounces, or 115 g each) (I like Meat District The O.G.)

4 large eggs

1 cup (158 g) white long-grain rice, cooked

(CONTINUED)

1. In a large pot over medium heat, heat the vegetable oil. Add the flour and stir constantly until there are no lumps. Continue stirring until the flour turns dark golden brown, about 10 minutes.

2. Add the celery, bell pepper, jalapeños, and onion. Mix well and cook for 10 minutes. Add the garlic and cook for 2 minutes more.

3. Slowly pour in the seafood stock a little at a time, stirring constantly. The mixture will thicken; add more or less stock based on how thick you prefer it. (If it gets too watery, you can add a cornstarch slurry to thicken.)

4. Add the shrimp, 1 tablespoon (12 g) of the Cajun seasoning, and the celery seed, paprika, and salt. Stir, cover, and let cook for 10 minutes. Add the green onions and set aside.

5. Season the patties with the remaining Cajun seasoning. On a griddle over medium-high heat, cook the patties to your desired doneness. Remove the patties and cook the eggs over easy.

6. Scoop rice on a plate and top with a heaping spoonful of the shrimp mixture. Top with a hamburger patty and finish with an egg. Repeat with the remaining ingredients.

CHORIPÁN WITH CAJUN CHIMICHURRI

YIELD: 4 sandwiches — PREP: 10 minutes — COOK: 25 minutes

Just about every part of the world has its own version of a sausage sandwich. Choripán is South America's spin. It's traditional street food that originated in Argentina, spreading throughout Chile, Peru, Bolivia, and beyond. The classic version is made with chorizo, but I wanted to change it up a little to put my own stamp on the classic. I make mine with andouille sausage because it has a deep rich flavor few sausages can match. I serve it up with a nod to my mom and her Cajun style—a chimichurri sauce that somehow manages to complement the sausage while bringing its own flavor fireworks to the party.

2 packages (16 ounces, or 455 g each) andouille smoked sausage

For the Cajun Chimichurri

1 bunch parsley, chopped

1 bunch cilantro, chopped

1 large red bell pepper, seeded and diced

2 cayenne peppers, minced

1 head garlic, peeled and minced

1 small shallot, peeled and minced

3 chipotle peppers in adobo sauce, chopped

Zest and juice of 1 large lemon

1 tablespoon (6 g) Italian seasoning

1 tablespoon (7 g) smoked paprika

1 tablespoon (8 g) coarse ground black pepper

2-3 tablespoons (24-36 g) Cajun seasoning

¼ cup (60 ml) red wine vinegar

1 cup (235 ml) extra-virgin olive oil

For the Sandwiches

1 large loaf artisan French bread (or substitute your favorite bread rolls)

1 package (16 ounces, or 455 g) sliced provolone cheese

1. Slice each sausage lengthwise, without cutting all the way through (the sausage should hinge open like a book).

2. Prepare the grill for medium-high heat. Grill the sausages open-face down until they are crosshatched with char marks, about 5 minutes. Flip and grill on the opposite side for the same amount of time.

3. In a medium bowl, combine the chimichurri ingredients and stir until completely mixed.

4. Cut the baguette into sections roughly the same length as the sausages. Cut each section in half lengthwise. Lay the sausage on one half of the bread and layer provolone slices on top of the sausage. Char the top of the cheese with a torch. (If you don't have a torch, place the sandwich under a broiler for 5 to 10 seconds.)

5. Spoon a mound of the chimichurri along the center of the cheese. Top with the other half of the bread, press down, and slice the sandwich in half. Repeat with the remaining sausages, bread, cheese, and chimichurri.

CAJUN SHRIMP LUMPIA

YIELD: 4 to 6 servings — PREP: 30 minutes — COOK: 15 minutes

Sometimes simpler is better. You don't need to dress this version of a lumpia up for it to be super satisfying. It's full of flavor, but it's also a light bite that can be the ideal starter for an outdoor cookout or as one superstar in a whole-table party spread. Either way, it is simple to put together and eats like a much more complicated dish. Pair it with a pale beer like summer ale, and you'll be one happy camper. Word to the wise, though: Fried lumpias don't keep well, so make as many as you and your crowd will eat at one sitting (you can, however, prepare them for frying beforehand).

For the Dipping Sauce

6 cloves garlic, peeled and minced fine

5 red Thai chili peppers, minced fine

⅓ cup (80 ml) cane vinegar

1 tablespoon (12 g) Cajun seasoning blend

For the Filling

1 pound (455 g) jumbo shrimp

2 tablespoons (24 g) Cajun seasoning blend

For the Lumpias

10–12 lumpia wrappers

2 cups (475 ml) vegetable oil

1. In a small bowl, combine all the ingredients for the dipping sauce. Mix well and set aside.

2. Peel and devein the shrimp, leaving the tail on. Cut a series of crosswise slits along the inside of each shrimp to release the natural curve. Season each shrimp liberally with the Cajun seasoning blend.

3. Fold over one corner of a lumpia wrapper. Lay a shrimp along the center of the fold with the tail hanging off the edge. Fold into an envelope shape and moisten the final corner before folding it over. Repeat with the remaining shrimp and wrappers.

4. Preheat the oil in a deep cast-iron skillet or pot over medium-high heat until the temperature reaches 350°F (180°C). Fry the lumpias in batches for 1 to 2 minutes each or until they are dark golden brown.

5. Transfer to a paper towel–lined plate and let rest for about 2 minutes or until the lumpias are cool enough to safely handle. Serve with the dipping sauce.

CAJUN SHRIMP AND ANDOUILLE SMASHBURGER

YIELD: 2 to 3 servings — PREP: 15 minutes — MARINATING: 15 minutes — COOK: 40 minutes

There's a reason why smashburgers are such a trend. By flattening a burger patty on a griddle, you increase the surface area that caramelizes. That's another way of saying that you boost the flavor into high gear. Smash the burgers right before they cook and you also increase the sear that locks in juices (it doesn't make sense to smash a burger after it's cooked because the opposite will happen). Long story short, if you want a killer burger with a crispy burst of flavor on the outside and tons of tasty juice on the inside, smashing it is the way to get there. An added benefit is that the burger stacks shorter, making even a double-patty sandwich easier to eat. The spicy shrimp and aioli I add to my version are the perfect complements to the perfect burger.

For the Cajun Aioli

½ cup (115 g) mayonnaise

1 tablespoon (14 g) garlic paste (or substitute [10 g] minced garlic)

Juice of ½ lemon

1 tablespoon (3 g) chopped fresh chives

1 tablespoon (15 ml) Louisiana pepper sauce

1 tablespoon (12 g) Creole seasoning mix

For the Smashburgers

½ pound (225 g) medium shrimp, peeled and deveined

2 tablespoons (28 ml) Creole-style injectable butter marinade

1 pound (455 g) uncooked andouille sausage

1 tablespoon (10 g) Creole no-salt seasoning blend, divided

¼ pound (115 g) Cajun cheese, sliced thick (I use Beehive Cheese Big John's Cajun.)

2 to 3 brioche buns

1. In a small bowl, combine the Cajun Aioli ingredients and mix thoroughly. Cover and refrigerate until you're ready to serve.

2. In a small bowl, combine the shrimp and Creole-style marinade. Toss to coat and set aside to marinate for at least 15 minutes. Form the sausage into 2 to 3 balls (remove it from the casings if you've purchased whole sausages).

3. Oil a hot griddle or cast-iron pan and cook the shrimp, sprinkling them with about half of the Creole no-salt seasoning blend. Cook just until they turn pink and begin to curl. Transfer to a plate.

4. Put the sausage balls on the griddle and smash them flat. Season them with the remaining Creole no-salt seasoning blend. Cook about 2 minutes each side or until the burger takes on a nice sear. After you flip the burgers, top with slices of the Cajun cheese and cover to speed the melting. Rest the patties for at least 3 minutes before preparing the sandwiches.

5. Toast both halves of the brioche buns. Smear the bottom half with a spoonful of the Cajun Aioli. Top with a burger, shrimp, and drip more Cajun Aioli on top. Press the top half of the bun down on the burger and slice in half. Repeat with remaining ingredients, serve hot, and enjoy!

CAJUN GARLIC ALFREDO WINGS

YIELD: 4 servings — PREP: 45 minutes — BRINING: 1 to 24 hours — COOK: 30 to 45 minutes

Welcome to a winning mashup of one of the best Italian pasta sauces with the best BBQ wings. I use a buttermilk brine for these beauties because it adds a deep rich flavor and tang to the chicken that shines through even after they are fried. The spicy tartness is the perfect contrast to a rich creamy sauce, and the balance of flavors and mouthfeel will blow your mind. Just start out slow when adding the Parmesan because it's easy to go heavy handed and make the sauce a little too cheesy and gluey, which will mask some of the magic of the spiced wings.

2 pounds (910 g) chicken wings

For the Brine

1 cup (235 ml) buttermilk

1 cup (235 ml) pickle juice

For the Dredge

2 cups (192 g) potato starch

1 teaspoon salt

1 teaspoon freshly ground black pepper

½ teaspoon garlic powder

1 teaspoon Cajun seasoning blend

2 cups (475 ml) vegetable oil

For the Cajun Alfredo Sauce

4 tablespoons (55 g) unsalted butter

1 head garlic, peeled and minced

1½ cups (355 ml) heavy cream (or substitute half-and-half)

1 tablespoon (12 g) Cajun seasoning

1 teaspoon smoked paprika

1 teaspoon ground cayenne pepper

1–2 cups (100–200 g) freshly grated Parmesan cheese

2 tablespoons (6 g) chopped fresh chives (for garnishing)

1. In large bowl, combine the buttermilk and pickle juice for the brine. Toss the wings in the brine and then cover and refrigerate for at least 1 hour and preferably overnight.

2. In a large bowl, whisk together the ingredients for the dredge. Remove the wings from the brine and drag through the dredge until completely coated.

3. Preheat about 1 inch (2.5 cm) of vegetable oil in a deep cast-iron skillet or pot to 325°F (170°C). Fry the wings in small batches for about 1 minute each side or until deep golden brown.

4. In large saucepan over medium-high heat, melt the butter for the Cajun Alfredo Sauce. Add the garlic and cook until lightly browned. Add the heavy cream and spices. Stir to combine. Add the Parmesan a little bit at a time until the sauce reaches your desired thickness. Remove the pan from the heat.

5. Toss the wings in the Cajun Alfredo Sauce. Sprinkle with the chives and enjoy.

SPICY CAJUN SKEWERS

YIELD: 4 servings — PREP: 10 minutes — COOK: 15 minutes

A lot of people like to use vegetables on their skewers, but for my money, those are speed bumps to the real flavor stars like the succulent seafood and spicy sausage in this recipe. I like this combination because the strong flavor of the classic sausage is a counterpoint to the richness of the shellfish. The best BBQ is all about balancing strong flavors like those. The spicy Cajun spin I put on these skewers adds another layer of zing, and the rub does double duty as the base for a basting sauce. Add these easy and quick-to-make skewers to your next cookout and find out for yourself.

For the Rub

1 tablespoon (9 g) garlic powder

1 tablespoon (6 g) Italian seasoning

1 tablespoon (7 g) paprika

1 tablespoon (5 g) ground cayenne pepper (Use less if you prefer milder.)

1 tablespoon (7 g) onion powder

1 tablespoon (6 g) coarse ground black pepper

1 tablespoon (18 g) salt

1 tablespoon (4 g) crushed red pepper flakes

For the Skewers

½ pound (225 g) Cajun andouille sausage, cut into 1-inch (2.5 cm) rounds

½ pound (225 g) jumbo shrimp, peeled and deveined

¼ pound (115 g) sea scallops

1–2 sticks (4–8 ounces, 112–225 g) unsalted butter (Use more if sauce is too thick.)

6 cloves garlic, peeled and minced

1. In a large bowl, whisk together the rub ingredients.

2. Skewer the proteins, starting with a sausage round and alternating sausage and shrimp or scallop. Dust each side of the skewers with about one-quarter of the rub.

3. In a small pot over medium heat, melt the butter and add the garlic. Cook for about 1 minute or long enough for the garlic to infuse the butter and then add the remaining rub. Stir and cook until fragrant.

4. Prepare a grill with the briquettes of your choice for medium-high heat. Grill the skewers for about 2 minutes on each side or until the shrimp turns opaque and begins to curl. Baste both sides with the butter sauce as the skewers grill. Serve when cooled enough to safely handle.

CRISPY CAJUN GARLIC DRUMSTICKS

YIELD: 4 servings — PREP: 10 minutes — COOK: 30 minutes

Much as I love me some wings, drumsticks come with their own handle. I like to butterfly the drumsticks because it increases the surface area that crisps up and cuts down on the cooking time. It also makes the drumsticks a much better platform for a complex spice mix like the Cajun blend I put on mine. The technique is easy. You just slice along the bone to the top of the drumstick and then splay out the meat—it's a little like spatchcocking a whole chicken. Don't be surprised if you bag the wings from now on and just go with butterflied drumsticks every time out; they're the ideal handheld BBQ hunger-killers.

For Drumsticks

1½ cups (360 g) pork panko (ground pork rinds)

4 large eggs

2 cups (250 g) all-purpose flour

Salt and pepper to taste

1 pound (455 g) chicken drumsticks

2 cups (475 ml) vegetable oil

For the Creamy Cajun Garlic Sauce

2 sticks (8 ounces, or 225 g) unsalted butter

½ cup (40 g) minced garlic

1 tablespoon (9 g) garlic powder

1 tablespoon (6 g) Italian seasoning

1 tablespoon (7 g) paprika

1 tablespoon (7 g) onion powder

1 tablespoon (6 g) coarse ground black pepper

1 tablespoon (4 g) crushed red pepper flakes

1 teaspoon salt

1 teaspoon ground cayenne pepper

1 cup (235 ml) heavy cream

1. Add the pork panko to a large shallow bowl. Whisk the eggs in a second large shallow bowl and whisk together the flour, salt, and pepper in a third bowl.

2. Butterfly each drumstick. Dredge each in the flour, then coat in the egg, and finally drag through the pork panko until completely coated. Repeat with the remaining drumsticks.

3. Preheat about 1 inch (2.5 cm) of vegetable oil in a deep cast-iron skillet to 325°F (170°C). Fry the drumsticks in small batches for 2 to 3 minutes each side until deep golden brown and the internal temperature reaches 165°F (74°C). Transfer the fried drumsticks to a large bowl.

4. In a small cast-iron pot over medium heat, combine the sauce ingredients. Cook for 5 minutes or until the butter is completely melted and all the spices are well incorporated.

5. Drizzle the drumsticks liberally with the sauce and serve hot.

CAJUN FOIL BOIL PACKS

YIELD: 4 servings — PREP: 15 minutes — COOK: 40 minutes

Spend a little time in Louisiana and you'll probably have the chance to enjoy a shrimp or crawfish boil, where they spread the seafood out on butcher paper–lined tables and let you go to town. Boil packs make that kind of feast a little bit more manageable, without losing any of the flavor or spicy Cajun authenticity. I like the contrast between the sweet flavor of the crab legs and the savory edge of the sausage. No bite of this meal is going to be boring, but you can always mix it up with your own favorite seafood or the catch of the day, like prawns, chicken, or even catfish, if that's your jam.

½ pound (225 g) frozen king crab legs

½ pound (225 g) medium shrimp

½ pound (225 g) sliced andouille sausage

1 bag (14 ounces, or 395 g) frozen mini corn cobs (usually 6 pieces)

4 cloves garlic, peeled and minced

1 tablespoon (15 ml) olive oil

2 tablespoons (20 g) Creole no-salt seasoning

2 tablespoons (24 g) spicy Creole seasoning

4 tablespoons (55 g) unsalted butter

1 lemon half

1 tablespoon (4 g) chopped fresh parsley

1. In a large bowl, combine the seafood, sausage, corn, garlic, oil, and seasonings. Toss the seafood to coat and then transfer to a large, resealable aluminum foil grilling bag with the butter.

2. Fire up your grill to medium-high (about 350°F, or 180°C). Grill the foil pack for 40 minutes.

3. Empty the pack into a large bowl or onto a large platter or sheet pan. Spritz with the lemon half and sprinkle with the parsley. Serve and enjoy!

WINGS EVERY WHICH WAY

Chicken wings are really kind of the Swiss Army knife of BBQ proteins. Born in Buffalo, New York, BBQ wings are super easy to cook and just as easy to get right. But most important to me, they are the ideal flavor canvasses. If a spice blend, marinade, or sauce works on wings, it will work on lots of other proteins, as well.

I regularly test out my new recipes on wings because they cook quickly and they don't require a lot of prep (or expense!). They also work with just about any texture you can imagine, from a sticky sweet sauce to air-fried crunchy perfection. If you like it on your tongue, chances are that it works on wings.

Well-cooked wings can also fit just about anywhere on the cookout table. They are great as appetizers, centerpiece party foods, handy snacks, and can even be the whole meal in a pinch. They are also perfect partners for beers of all kinds. I drink an India pale ale when I'm prepping, and I find that a plain-old light beer is perfect for cutting through a heavy smoke or spice flavor when eating the wings.

It's hard to go wrong with however you cook your wings, but for best results, be careful to buy the freshest wings possible. They shouldn't have any odor to speak of, and keep an eye out for freezer burn if you are buying in bulk. I find I get the best wings at my local butcher shop. But you can buy fresh, clean wings at just about any well-stocked supermarket.

For ease of use, I've organized the recipes in this chapter under the way the wings are cooked I hope that helps you find exactly the wings you want to make tonight!

SPICY FISH SAUCE WINGS

YIELD: 2 servings — PREP: 10 minutes — MARINATING: 1 to 24 hours — COOK: 40 minutes

If you've ever tasted fish sauce by itself, you might have been turned off by the flavor. Don't judge all dishes by that experience. Fish sauce is a condiment and widely used in really fantastic ways in Filipino cooking. I like to add it sparingly to my BBQ. The great thing about combining so many strong flavors in a BBQ dish like this one is that no single flavor will run away and overpower the whole recipe. They work together nicely. So, suspend your judgement, embrace the fish sauce, and find your way to new flavor frontiers. I promise, you'll be glad you did.

For the Wings

1 cup (200 g) granulated sugar

1 cup (235 ml) fish sauce

1 pound (455 g) chicken wings

2 cups (384 g) potato starch

2 cups (475 ml) peanut oil

For the Sauce

2 tablespoons (28 ml) olive oil

1 head garlic, peeled and minced

2–3 Thai chilies, diced

5 scallions, diced

1–2 tablespoons (15–28 ml) fish sauce

1. In a large bowl, whisk together the sugar and fish sauce. Add the chicken wings and toss until they are completely coated. Cover and marinate for at least 1 hour and preferably overnight. Or you can use a chamber vacuum sealer on instant marinate function (times three) for much quicker marination.

2. Add the potato starch to a large shallow bowl. Transfer the wings from the marinade into the potato starch, dredging them until they are completely coated.

3. Preheat the peanut oil in a deep cast-iron skillet or pot to 300°F (150°C). Fry the wings in batches for 8 to 10 minutes or until the chicken's internal temperature reaches 165°F (74°C). Remove the wings and increase the oil heat to 350°F (180°C). Fry the wings for 1 minute more to make them extra crispy. Transfer the wings to a large bowl.

4. In a small cast-iron pan, heat the olive oil and add the garlic for the sauce. Cook until the garlic begins to brown. Add the Thai chilies, scallions, and fish sauce. Stir to mix thoroughly and cook for about 2 minutes or until heated through and bubbling.

5. Pour the sauce over the wings and toss to coat. Serve and enjoy!

CREAMY CAJUN GARLIC WINGS

YIELD: 4 servings — PREP: 15 minutes — COOK: 45 minutes

Combining cream with Cajun spices may not seem like the most natural marriage ever, but you might be surprised at how well it works. The cream base helps to glue the spices to the chicken and cools some of the spicy bite a shade. You can also use milk or half-and-half, but personally, I love the rich, full-bodied mouthfeel of real cream. Once you find out how well the sauce works, you might want to try it on other proteins and cuts. It does wonders for fried catfish, and I like it on chicken thighs as well. You can even use it to dress up grilled veggies and add a unique twist to them.

For the Wings

2 pounds (910 g) chicken wings

1 teaspoon salt

1 teaspoon coarse ground black pepper

1 teaspoon garlic powder

1 cup (125 g) all-purpose flour

2 cups (475 ml) peanut oil

For the Creamy Cajun Garlic Sauce

8 tablespoons (112 g) unsalted butter

½ cup (48 g) minced garlic

1 tablespoon (9 g) garlic powder

1 tablespoon (6 g) Italian seasoning

1 tablespoon (7 g) paprika

1 tablespoon (5 g) ground cayenne pepper

1 tablespoon (7 g) onion powder

1 tablespoon (6 g) coarse ground black pepper

1 teaspoon salt

1 tablespoon (4 g) crushed red pepper flakes

1 cup (235 ml) heavy cream

2 tablespoons (6 g) chopped fresh chives

1. In a large bowl, lightly season the wings with the salt, pepper, and garlic powder (you can use an SPG seasoning blend for this, if you keep one on hand). Place the flour in a large shallow bowl. Drag the wings through the flour until they're coated.

2. Preheat the peanut oil in a deep cast-iron skillet or pot to 300°F (150°C). Fry the wings in batches for 8 to 10 minutes until golden brown or until the internal temperature reaches 165°F (74°C). Transfer the wings to a large bowl.

3. In a small cast-iron pot over medium heat, melt the butter for the sauce. Add the garlic and cook for 3 to 5 minutes or until dark golden brown. Add all the seasonings and cook for 2 to 3 minutes more until fragrant.

4. Add the heavy cream a little at a time until you achieve your preferred thickness. Pour the sauce over the wings and garnish with the chives or serve the sauce on the side as a dip.

BLOODY MARY WINGS

YIELD: 4 servings — PREP: 1 hour — MARINATING: 1 hour — COOK: 1 hour

Here's the thing about Bloody Marys: They're a brunch favorite because you can add so many flavors to them, and they support absurdly intricate garnishes. I've seen them served up with slab-cut bacon skewers, prawns, all kinds of vegetables, and everything but the kitchen sink. Homemade Bloody Mary mix is ripe with spices, which makes the cocktail perfect as the inspiration for unique chicken wings full of eye-opening spices and a little bit of alcoholic zing. The aioli in this recipe is a simple dip that cuts some of the heat in the wings and adds just a little bit of a tart note to the dish.

For the Wings

1 pound (455 g) chicken wings

2 tablespoons (28 ml) olive oil

**For the Seasoning Rub
and Marinade**

1 teaspoon celery seed

1 teaspoon garlic powder

1 teaspoon kosher salt

1 teaspoon coarse ground black pepper

1 cup (235 ml) Bloody Mary mix (I prefer
    Bear & Burton's Key West Style Mary Mix.)

¼ cup (60 ml) vodka

For the Basting Sauce

½ cup (120 ml) Bloody Mary mix

¼ cup (60 ml) vodka

For the Dill Pickle Aioli

½ cup (115 g) mayonnaise

1 teaspoon chopped fresh dill

1 tablespoon (14 g) garlic paste

2 tablespoons (28 ml) dill pickle juice

Juice ½ lemon

Pinch salt and pepper

1. Place the wings into an aluminum roasting pan and drizzle with olive oil. Toss until entirely coated. Sprinkle the celery seed, garlic powder, salt, and pepper over the wings and then toss the wings until they're covered all over with the seasonings.

2. Pour the Bloody Mary mix and vodka over the wings and mix thoroughly. Cover and refrigerate for 1 hour.

3. In a small cast-iron pot, combine the Bloody Mary mix and vodka for the basting sauce. Preheat your grill with briquettes piled to one side and to high heat, about 400°F (200°C). Add applewood chunks to the coals.

4. Transfer the wings and the pot with the basting sauce onto the grill and smoke in indirect heat for 45 minutes or until the wings reach an internal temperature of 180°F (82°C). Check frequently to avoid burning the wings or the sauce.

5. While the wings are cooking, combine the aioli ingredients in a small bowl and mix well until completely emulsified.

6. After about 40 minutes or when the sauce is reduced by half, use the basting sauce to liberally baste the wings. Close the lid and finish smoking the wings. Remove the wings, serve with the aioli, and enjoy!

SINIGANG WINGS

YIELD: 4 servings — **PREP: 15 minutes** — **MARINATING: 1 hour** — **COOK: 1 hour**

Sinigang is another Filipino classic I've adopted to BBQ. It's traditionally used as the sour soup flavoring based on ingredients like tamarind. I use the mix to give wings a powerhouse unusual taste. The packaged spice blend makes prep easy and quick, and a little applewood in the smoker adds a nice depth of smoky flavor to the wings. You can find sinigang mix at most Asian markets or through many online stores. It's a wonderfully different blend to add into stews, onto grilled meats, and more. Channel your inner Filipino and find your own uses for it!

For the Wings

2 pounds (910 g) chicken wings

3 tablespoons (45 ml) fish sauce

½ packet (1½ ounces, or 40 g) sinigang sa sampalok mix (Tamarind soup mix)

For the Sinigang Sauce

¾ cup (175 ml) water

5 cloves garlic, peeled and minced

½ cup (100 g) granulated sugar

½ packet (1½ ounces, or 40 g) sinigang sa sampalok mix

1–2 tablespoons (4–8 g) crushed red pepper flakes

3 tablespoons (18 g) chopped scallions

1. In a large bowl, dress the chicken wings with the fish sauce. Sprinkle with the sinigang mix and toss until completely coated. Cover and refrigerate for 1 hour or place in a chamber vacuum sealer on instant marinate function for quicker marination.

2. Prepare a smoker with applewood, preheated to 350°F (180°C). Smoke the wings for about 1 hour or until their internal temperature reaches 180°F (82°C).

3. In a large pan over low heat, combine the sauce ingredients. Cook until the sugar is completely dissolved and the sauce has thickened slightly. (Do not cook over high heat or for too long or the sugar will burn; the sauce only needs a few minutes to cook.)

4. In a large bowl, combine the wings and sauce, reserving about one-quarter of the sauce. Toss until completely coated. Drizzle with remaining sauce and scallions and serve.

GARLIC LEMON PEPPER WINGS

YIELD: 2 servings — PREP: 10 minutes — COOK: 1 hour

Sometimes, simple and light is just the answer to what you're craving. These wings deliver with the closest smoky goodness you can get to a palate cleanser. This straightforward recipe takes precious little time and effort to whip together, leaving you plenty of the afternoon to work on the rest of the cookout spread. It's also the perfect complement to heavier, more traditional backyard get-together favorites. No matter when you make and serve them, though, you'll enjoy a refreshing zing that will wake up your taste buds for further adventures. These are ideal with a light or sweet drink, like iced tea or a pale summer ale.

1 pound (455 g) chicken wings

2 tablespoons (28 ml) olive oil

Salt and pepper to taste

1 lemon

2 tablespoons (28 g) unsalted butter

1 head garlic, peeled and minced

2–3 tablespoons (24–36 g) lemon pepper, plus more as needed

1. Prepare a grill with applewood chips for medium heat and indirect cooking to about 300°F (150°C).

2. In a large bowl, drizzle the olive oil over the wings and toss until thoroughly coated. Season liberally with salt and pepper.

3. Smoke the wings indirectly for about 45 minutes or until they are rich golden brown and still a little shiny. Move the wings directly over the coals, smoking them for 2 to 3 minutes more per side or until they take on a nice char and reach an internal temperature of at least 165°F (74°C). I like to cook mine to 190°F (88°C). When done, transfer the wings to a large bowl.

4. Preheat a cast-iron pan over the coals. Zest the lemon and set the zest aside. Cut the lemon in half and place face down on the grill. Add the butter to the pan. When it's melted, add the garlic and cook for about 5 minutes or until browned.

5. Add the lemon pepper to the pan and squeeze the juice from the grilled lemon halves into the pan. Stir to combine and cook for 5 minutes more.

6. Pour the butter mix over the wings and toss until completely coated. Sprinkle with the lemon zest and a little more lemon pepper and enjoy!

TOCINO WINGS

YIELD: 4 servings — PREP: 10 minutes — MARINATING: 24 to 48 hours — COOK: 30 minutes

Tocino is Spanish for "bacon," and in Spain, they usually make tocino dishes with cubed pork belly. In the Philippines, they put their own spin on it, like I did with this tasty dish. I based these wings on the tocino flavors that are common in Filipino cooking, and I've listed all the trimmings. That includes an egg because Filipinos often make and eat tocino recipes for breakfast. I've also included the red food coloring regularly used by native Filipinos to create a signature look. I prefer completely natural food coloring and that's what I always use. It costs a little more, but artificial versions can sometimes give food a weird chemical aftertaste. Of course, if you prefer, you can just leave the food coloring out.

For the Marinade

½ cup (115 g) packed light brown sugar

1 tablespoon (14 g) kosher salt

1 tablespoon (8 g) coarse ground black pepper

8 cloves garlic, peeled and finely minced

1 tablespoon (15 ml) soy sauce

2 tablespoons (30 ml) cane vinegar

½ cup (120 ml) 100 percent mango juice (or substitute pineapple or apple juice)

2–3 drops natural red food coloring (optional)

For the Wings

2 pounds (910 g) chicken wings

1 tablespoon (15 g) rice flour (optional, for crispier wings)

Garlic fried rice (optional)

1 egg, sunny-side up (optional)

Crispy fried garlic (optional)

1. Combine all the marinade ingredients in a large plastic container with a lid. Mix thoroughly. Add the wings and toss until completely coated. Cover and refrigerate at least overnight, but preferably for 48 hours.

2. Prepare the grill with your favorite briquettes to about 350°F (180°C). Dredge the wings in rice flour if you prefer a crispier texture.

3. Grill the wings directly over the coals for 8 to 10 minutes per side or until they are nicely charred. Then, move the wings off to the side out of direct heat and cook until the internal temperature reaches 180°F (82°C).

4. If you prefer the full dish, serve over garlic fried rice and top with an egg sunny-side up. Garnish with crispy fried garlic.

JALAPEÑO LIME WINGS

YIELD: 4 servings — PREP: 10 minutes — COOK: 40 minutes

Need an excuse to mix up a pitcher of margaritas? Here you go. These hot-weather wings serve up equal parts spicy bite and refreshing tartness in a crusty grilled taste sensation. The dish is all about light and bright flavors, complemented by a simple Mexican classic dip of cilantro and crema Mexicana. Crema Mexicana is a south-of-the-border version of sour cream, but thicker and richer. Try it once, and you'll end up using it in a lot of different recipes. It's perfect for cutting the heavy grilled goodness of these wings. Of course, if that just isn't your jam, go ahead and substitute your favorite ranch or blue cheese dip. It's all good!

For the Wings

2 pounds (910 g) chicken wings

1 teaspoon salt

1 teaspoon freshly ground black pepper

For the Sauce

4 tablespoons (55 g) salted butter

2 jalapeños, diced

1 tablespoon (10 g) minced roasted garlic (or substitute raw garlic)

Zest and juice of 1 large lime

For Serving

2 tablespoons (2 g) cilantro, chopped

3 tablespoons (45 g) crema Mexicana

1. In a large bowl, season the wings liberally with the salt and pepper.

2. Prepare a grill with briquettes on one side only to about 400°F (200°C). Grill the wings in indirect heat for 30 to 40 minutes or until they have taken on a dark brown crust and the internal temperature reaches at least 165°F (74°C). I like to cook mine to 190°F (88°C).

3. In a small cast-iron pot directly over the coals, melt the butter for the sauce. Add the remaining sauce ingredients and cook for 5 minutes.

4. Transfer the wings to a large bowl and top with the sauce. Toss until completely coated. Top with the cilantro and crema Mexicana and enjoy!

BUFFALO WINGS ON STEROIDS

YIELD: 4 servings — PREP: 15 minutes — COOK: 40 minutes

By the time you're done making these, the meat should be barely holding onto the bone. That tenderness, along with a punch-you-in-the-face combination of flavors, makes this a super memorable addition to any meal and especially as the center of a game-day spread. My not-so-secret secret is dusting the wings with cornstarch before grilling. That guarantees a satisfyingly crunchy skin that traps all those flavorful juices inside where they belong. I've included my Blue Cheese Dip here, which is perfect with the wings but also great with vegetables, chips, lumpias, and other dippables.

For the Wings

2 pounds (910 g) chicken wings

¼ cup (60 ml) olive oil

2 tablespoons (16 g) cornstarch

For the Rub

2 teaspoons salt

1 teaspoon freshly ground black pepper

2 teaspoons garlic powder

For the Blue Cheese Dip

1 cup (120 g) blue cheese crumbles

¼ cup (60 g) sour cream

¼ cup (60 g) mayonnaise

½ cup (120 ml) buttermilk

1 teaspoon lemon juice

1 teaspoon kosher salt

1 teaspoon coarse ground black pepper

1 teaspoon garlic powder

1 teaspoon ground cayenne pepper

1 teaspoon smoked paprika

For the Sauce

¼ cup (60 ml) olive oil

5 cloves garlic, peeled and minced

1 tablespoon (4 g) crushed red chili flakes

1 tablespoon (12 g) everything bagel seasoning

1 tablespoon (18 g) BBQ sauce (I use Blazing Star Original BBQ Sauce.)

½ cup (120 ml) buffalo wing sauce (I use Tacticalories HELLDIVER Buffalo Wing Sauce.)

1 tablespoon (12 g) spicy BBQ rub (I go with Blazing Star Reaper Rub and Seasoning.)

2 tablespoons (28 g) salted butter

1. Pat the wings dry. Whisk together all the rub ingredients. Toss the wings in olive oil and coat with the rub. Dust lightly with cornstarch, which will make the wings crispier.

2. Prepare a grill with your favorite briquettes heated to about 300°F (150°C). Grill the wings for 10 minutes, flipping three times during grilling. (Adjust the time for your preferred doneness.)

3. In a large bowl, combine all the ingredients for the Blue Cheese Dip and stir until completely mixed. Cover and refrigerate until ready to serve.

4. Heat the olive oil for the sauce in a cast-iron saucepot over medium heat. Add the garlic, chili flakes, and everything bagel seasoning. Cook, stirring, until aromatic and browned.

5. Add the BBQ sauce, buffalo wing sauce, BBQ rub, and butter. Stir to combine and cook until heated and emulsified. Toss the wings in the sauce until completely coated. Serve with the Blue Cheese Dip.

CAJUN HONEY BUTTER WINGS

YIELD: 4 servings — PREP: 15 minutes — COOK: 45 to 60 minutes

Honey and Cajun spices go together like peanut butter and jam. Maybe better. There is something about the unique blend of spices that begs to be paired with something naturally thick and sweet, and honey sure does the trick. A key to this recipe, and many of my wing creations, is to cook the chicken indirectly. Moving these delicate parts of the bird out of the path of direct heat means that you can cook them long enough to really infuse them with the smoke, without fear of completely drying them out.

For the Wings

2 pounds (910 g) chicken wings

½ teaspoon salt

1 teaspoon coarse ground black pepper

2 teaspoons Italian seasoning

½ cup (64 g) cornstarch

For the Sauce

6 tablespoons (85 g) unsalted butter, room temperature

¼ cup (40 g) minced garlic

2 teaspoons garlic powder

2 teaspoons smoked paprika

1 teaspoon ground cayenne pepper

2 teaspoons onion powder

½ teaspoon crushed red pepper flakes

3 tablespoons (60 g) honey

1. In a large bowl, combine the wings with the salt, pepper, and Italian seasoning. Add the cornstarch and toss until the wings are coated all over. (The cornstarch guarantees the wings end up crispy.)

2. Prepare the grill with briquettes topped by applewood chunks, heated to about 400°F (200°C). Arrange the wings to cook in indirect heat.

3. In a small cast-iron pot over medium heat, melt the butter for the sauce. Add the garlic and cook for 5 minutes. Add the seasonings and stir until completely combined. Cook for 5 minutes more and then add the honey and turn off the heat.

4. After 45 to 60 minutes, or when the wings are deep brown with an internal temperature of at least 165°F (74°C), transfer the wings to a large bowl. Pour the sauce over the wings and toss to coat. Serve and enjoy!

SALT-AND-VINEGAR WINGS

YIELD: 4 servings — PREP: 10 minutes — MARINATING: 4 to 24 hours — COOK: 1 hour

This dish has a little bit of a "fish and chips" vibe. There's just something about the combination of vinegar and salt that seems to make anything—from potato chips to chicken wings—better. I add ranch dressing to the marinade to build in even more layers of flavor and because the coolness of the dressing perfectly complements the vinegar in the recipe. Although you can substitute other types of vinegar, I'd stick with cane vinegar if you can find it. It's a staple of Filipino cooking thanks to a complex flavor that is a little like sherry vinegar, but incredibly unique. It's made from sugar cane, and I always keep a bottle on hand because it adds a special sour note to savory sauces.

For the Marinade

½ cup (120 ml) distilled white vinegar

½ cup (120 ml) cane vinegar (or substitute apple cider vinegar)

1 teaspoon granulated sugar

1 teaspoon garlic powder

1 tablespoon (10 g) ranch seasoning mix (I prefer Hidden Valley Original Ranch Seasoning & Salad Dressing Mix.)

2 tablespoons (36 g) sea salt (I recommend Osmo Flakey White Sea Salt.)

For the Wings

2 pounds (910 g) chicken wings

2½ teaspoons baking powder

1 teaspoon kosher salt

2 tablespoons (6 g) chopped fresh chives

1. In a Mason jar, combine the marinade ingredients. Shake vigorously until the sugar and salt are completely dissolved.

2. Pat the wings dry and transfer to a large, gallon-size (3.8 L) resealable kitchen bag. Add about three-quarters of the marinade and mix well. Refrigerate for at least 4 hours, but preferably overnight. Place the remaining marinade in the fridge until needed later.

3. Prepare the smoker with your favorite wood, preheated to 250°F (120°C).

4. Remove the wings from the bag and pat dry. Transfer to a large bowl and sprinkle with the baking powder and kosher salt. Toss until completely coated.

5. Transfer the wings to a wire rack. Smoke them for 30 minutes.

6. Increase the smoker temperature to 425°F (220°F) and smoke the wings for 20 to 30 minutes more or until golden brown and the internal temperature is at least 175°F (79°C), or 190°F to 200°F (88°C to 93°C) if you want extra crispy wings.

7. Transfer the wings to a large bowl. Drizzle with the reserved marinade and sprinkle with a bit more sea salt and the chives. Serve immediately and enjoy!

GARLIC CHILI OIL WINGS

YIELD: 4 to 6 servings — PREP: 10 minutes — COOK: 45 to 60 minutes

You can usually judge great wings by the napkin factor: If you use up half a stack working your way through the plate, the dish is a true winner. This recipe might take up a whole stack. The over-the-top sticky factor is thanks to a homemade garlic chili oil that leans heavy on the garlic as a base on which all the other flavors are built. The flavor profile is uniquely Asian; the combination of garlic and chili flakes is common in Filipino cooking, but you'll also recognize it from your favorite Chinese takeout. The great thing about that familiar tasty blend is that it never grows old and neither do these wings. Just be sure to stock up on napkins—you're going to need them!

For the Wings

2–3 pounds (910 g–1.4 kg) chicken wings

¼ cup (48 g) spicy BBQ rub (I use Blazing Star Reaper Rub and Seasoning.)

2 tablespoons (16 g) cornstarch (optional)

For the Garlic Chili Oil

1 head garlic, peeled and minced

2 tablespoons (20 g) minced shallots

½ cup (32 g) Szechuan chili flakes

2 tablespoons (8 g) red pepper flakes

1 tablespoon (15 ml) sesame oil

1 teaspoon kosher salt

½ cup (120 ml) canola oil

Sea salt (optional)

1. Prepare the smoker or grill with your favorite wood, heated to 250°F (120°C).

2. Place the wings in a large bowl and season liberally with the BBQ rub-and-seasoning mix. Dust with the cornstarch (optional, for extra crispiness). Toss and mix until the wings are completely coated.

3. Smoke the wings for 45 to 60 minutes or until they are dark golden brown and the internal temperature reaches 190°F (88°C).

4. In a large heat-safe bowl, combine the Garlic Chili Oil ingredients, except for the canola oil. Mix well. In a small cast-iron pot over high heat, bring the canola oil to a boil. Pour it over the dry ingredients and allow to steep for 2 minutes. Stir until thoroughly mixed.

5. Transfer the wings to a large bowl and drizzle with the Garlic Chili Oil. Toss until completely coated. Season with sea salt, if desired. Serve hot.

HABANERO CHIMICHURRI WINGS

YIELD: 4 servings — PREP: 10 minutes — COOK: 40 minutes

Take a moment to appreciate the humble habanero. It's not all about the heat with this one. Habaneros also bring some subtle flavors, but it's important to buy mature peppers; the green are immature. The bonus is that they come in beautiful shades of red, orange, and yellow, and there are new varieties all the time. There is even a chocolate habanero, which might be a good choice to try out in a chimichurri like the one in this recipe. The blast of heat from the pepper is the ideal complement for the other tart and herbal notes in the sauce and really elevates the simple chicken wing.

For the Chimichurri

1 head garlic, peeled and minced

1 cup (64 g) minced fresh parsley

1 cup (16 g) minced cilantro

1 shallot, peeled and minced

2 habanero peppers, minced

Juice of 1 lime

¼ cup (60 ml) red wine vinegar

1 tablespoon (9 g) garlic powder

1 tablespoon (8 g) coarse ground black pepper

1 tablespoon (7 g) smoked paprika

1 tablespoon (14 g) kosher salt

½ cup (120 ml) olive oil

2 pounds (910 g) chicken wings

1. In a large bowl, combine all the chimichurri ingredients and mix thoroughly.

2. Prepare a grill with the briquettes in the center, heated to about 400°F (200°C). Grill the wings arranged around the edges of the grate for 30 to 40 minutes or until the wings are dark brown and crispy and the internal temperature reaches at least 165°F (74°C). I like to cook mine to 190°F (88°C).

3. Transfer the wings to a large bowl and cover with the chimichurri. Toss until completely coated and serve hot.

HONEY GARLIC TEQUILA LIME WINGS

YIELD: 4 to 6 servings — PREP: 15 minutes — COOK: 60 to 90 minutes

A little boozy cooking can be a great way to cut through summer heat and make the most of flavors you might not use all the time. A quality tequila gives these wings an interesting complexity and their own unique sting, and heating it burns off some of the alcohol. Honey mellows everything out, and lime and tequila are the best of friends. All the ingredients work in perfect harmony in this dish. Don't forget to make yourself a little summer cocktail to go with the wings. After all, the bottle's already open!

For the Wings

2–3 pounds (910 g–1.4 kg) chicken wings

2 tablespoons (28 ml) olive oil

1 tablespoon (18 g) sea salt

1 tablespoon (8 g) coarse ground black pepper

1 teaspoon garlic powder

¼ cup (23 g) chimichurri dry rub (I like Al Frugoni Chimichurri Seasoning The Original.)

For the Sauce

½ cup (112 g) salted butter

1 head garlic, peeled and minced

Juice and zest of 1 lime

1 shot (1½ ounces, or 42 ml) tequila (I use Clase Azul.)

½ cup (160 g) spicy honey, plus more as needed (I use Mike's Hot Honey.)

1. In a large bowl, drizzle the chicken wings with olive oil and toss to coat. Cover with the salt, pepper, garlic powder (you can use an SPG mix if you have one on hand), and the chimichurri dry rub. Toss until the wings are completely and evenly coated with the dry ingredients.

2. Prepare the smoker with the wood of your choice to medium heat (about 300°F, or 150°C). Smoke the chicken wings for 1 to 1½ hours or until the internal temperature reaches 195°F (91°C).

3. In a small cast-iron pot over low heat, melt the butter for the sauce. Add the garlic, lime juice, tequila, and honey and stir well until completely combined. Cook for 5 minutes.

4. Transfer the wings to a large bowl, top with the sauce, and toss until coated all over. Drizzle with a little more honey, sprinkle with the lime zest, and serve.

49ER (HONEY BUTTER SRIRACHA) WINGS

YIELD: 4 servings — PREP: 15 minutes — COOK: 1 hour

I named this one for all those miners who made their way to California for the gold rush in the 1850s (well, and also as a nod to my favorite football team). They were crazy for gold, and this recipe honors the inevitable attraction to the king of metals . . . with actual edible gold dust (you can leave it off if food bling just ain't your thing; the flavor remains the same either way). The carefully balanced sriracha coating is just about as valuable as the gold and more satisfying on the tongue. All in all, this recipe is loaded with salty, savory, sweet, and a whole lot more. One bite and you'll think you've struck your own treasure.

2 pounds (910 g) chicken wings

8 tablespoons (112 g) unsalted butter

2 tablespoons (18 g) sriracha rub

2 tablespoons (28 g) garlic paste

¼ cup (60 ml) sriracha sauce

⅓ cup (115 g) honey

1 tablespoon (15 ml) soy sauce

1 teaspoon lime juice

Natural red food coloring (optional)

Black flakey salt to taste (optional)

24k edible gold dust (optional)

1. Let the wings sit out and come to room temperature. In a small cast-iron pot, melt the butter. Dress the wings with 3 tablespoons (45 ml) of the butter (set aside the remaining butter in the pot).

2. In a large bowl, dust the wings with the sriracha rub. Toss until they are evenly coated.

3. Prepare the smoker with applewood and heat to about 450°F (230°F). Smoke the wings for 40 to 45 minutes or until they reach an internal temperature of 190°F (88°C).

4. Reheat the remaining butter over low heat and add the garlic paste, sriracha sauce, honey, soy sauce, and lime juice. Stir in red food coloring if desired.

5. Transfer the wings to a large bowl. Dress with the sauce and toss until well coated. Dust the wings with the black flakey salt and a tiny amount of the edible gold dust, if using. Serve hot and enjoy!

SMOKED AND FRIED BUFFALO TURKEY WINGS

YIELD: 4 servings — PREP: 20 minutes — COOK: 1 hour

A lot of people only encounter a turkey wing when they carve it off the whole bird on Thanksgiving. That's a shame because there is a ton of potential with this bird part. The turkey wing is usually broken down at the joints of the wing to create a drumette (closest to the body), a "flat," which looks like an overlarge chicken wing, and the wing tip, which is used less often. Turkey wing meat is richer and more complex in flavor than chicken wings, with a noticeably more robust texture. Although it's white meat, the flavor is closer to dark meat. The cut is also inexpensive and can easily be prepared in any way you would cook a chicken wing.

For the Wings

2 large turkey wings (4 ounces, or 115 g each)

1 tablespoon (12 g) BBQ rub

½ cup (64 g) cornstarch

For the Sauce

4 tablespoons (55 g) salted butter

1 tablespoon (10 g) minced garlic

1 cup (235 ml) buffalo wing sauce (I use Blazing Star Original BBQ Sauce.)

1 tablespoon (12 g) spicy BBQ rub (I use Blazing Star Reaper Rub and Seasoning.)

2 cups (475 ml) peanut oil

1. Break down the turkey wings by cutting them at the joints (or have your butcher do this). Season liberally with the BBQ rub and then sprinkle with the cornstarch. Toss until completely coated.

2. Prepare a grill with applewood and heat to 350°F (180°C). Place the turkey wings on the grill in indirect heat. Grill the turkey for about 1 hour or until the internal temperature reaches 165°F (74°C).

3. While the wings cook, make the sauce. In a small cast-iron pot over medium-high heat, melt the butter. Add the garlic and cook for 5 minutes. Add the buffalo wing sauce and stir to combine. Whisk in the spicy BBQ rub and cook until the sauce is slightly thickened. Turn off the heat.

4. In a deep cast-iron skillet or pot, preheat about ½ inch (1.3 cm) of peanut oil to 350°F (180°C). Fry the smoked turkey wings one at a time for about 1 minute or just until crispy and slightly charred.

5. Serve the wings hot, drizzled with the sauce. Enjoy!

STICKY ADOBO WINGS

YIELD: 4 servings — PREP: 30 minutes — COOK: 90 minutes

You may be familiar with adobo Mexican-style or the way the Spanish make it. Filipino adobo is unique. It offers an intriguing mix of spices that is equal parts sweet, hot, and sour. The style traditionally leans on a little vinegar and soy sauce and can include tropical flavors. I use coconut vinegar for this dish, but the two elements could easily be separated to enhance the tropical flavor. No matter what, though, Filipino adobo leaves room for experimentation because it's so accommodating of adaptation. You can go a little tangier or use the common ingredient of whole peppercorns to boost the peppery goodness (try using tri-color peppercorns for a subtle addition to the flavor profile of the dish).

For the Wings

2 pounds (910 g) chicken wings

¼ cup (32 g) cornstarch

2 tablespoons (28 ml) peanut oil

For the Sauce

⅓ cup (80 ml) soy sauce

⅓ cup (80 ml) coconut vinegar (or substitute white vinegar)

⅓ cup (80 ml) water

3 tablespoons (39 g) granulated sugar

2 bay leaves

6 cloves garlic, peeled and minced

2 tablespoons (12 g) peeled and minced fresh ginger

1 teaspoon coarse ground black pepper

For Serving

2 cups (14 ounces, or 396 g) long-grain white rice, cooked

1 tablespoon (6 g) crispy fried garlic (optional)

1 tablespoon (6 g) chopped green onions (optional)

1. Pat the chicken wings dry. In a large bowl, combine the wings and cornstarch and toss until the wings are coated all over (this is going to up the crispiness without affecting the flavor).

2. In a large nonstick skillet or an enameled Dutch oven, preheat the peanut oil over medium heat to about 350°F (180°C). Fry the wings in batches until just golden brown, about 10 minutes. Turn the wings once during frying. Don't overcrowd the pan or the oil will cool and the wings will be greasy.

3. Return all the wings to the skillet or Dutch oven and add all the ingredients for the sauce. Bring to a simmer, cover, and cook over medium heat for 8 minutes, stirring halfway through.

4. Increase the heat to medium-high, uncover, and continue cooking, stirring occasionally until the sauce thickens into a glaze and the wings are fully cooked, about 8 minutes more. Remove the bay leaves from the sauce.

5. Serve the chicken on a bed of the white rice, drizzled with the sauce. Sprinkle with crispy fried garlic and green onions, if desired. Serve and enjoy.

PARTY FOOD

To me, BBQ is the foundation of almost every great party. Growing up in Hayward, California, birthday parties, holiday celebrations, and get-togethers of all kinds revolved around backyard cookouts. Outside of San Francisco itself, Bay Area days are warm without getting too hot, and the nights cool off just enough for you to need a hoodie or a sweater. Backyard parties last a long time, and the flavors need to be memorable.

That's why my fondest family memories are of large backyard parties with the smell of grilling meat and chicken, a backdrop of music, and a table full of the type of food you can hold and eat while you're talking and laughing.

In short, we're talking party food.

Although most party food recipes could be appetizers in another setting, they are all about offering a variety of flavors and textures for a celebration. The idea is to have lots of different things to try on one plate. Or people can just grab a single piece of food and pop it into their mouth. Call it drive-by eating.

My party food favorites work perfectly as stand-alone snacks or as part of a much bigger ensemble. Each bite should offer something a little bit unique, but that works with other foods. Fill the table and fill the plate. Now you're partying!

GARLIC BUTTER STEAK BITES

YIELD: 4 servings — PREP: 10 minutes — COOK: 40 minutes

The word that always comes up when I serve these premium beef appetizers is "addictive." Start with one-of-a-kind meat, and it's hard to go wrong. That's why I use Wagyu in my steak bites, and you should too. I coat them with tallow spray rather than vegetable oil to bring out the rich, deep flavor of the beef. You don't need much beyond that flavor to wind up with a wholly satisfying meal in one bite.

1 package (1½ pounds, or 680 g) American Wagyu beef teres major (shoulder tender)

Wagyu beef tallow spray (I use South Chicago Packing Wagyu Beef Tallow Spray.)

½ cup (96 g) garlic jalapeño BBQ seasoning rub (I use Kosmos Q The Best Garlic Jalapeno Rub.)

5 cloves garlic, peeled and chopped

3 tablespoons (42 g) unsalted butter

1 tablespoon (18 g) sea salt

1 tablespoon (4 g) coarsely chopped fresh parsley

1. Slice the Wagyu beef into medallions. Transfer to a large bowl and spray liberally with the beef tallow spray. Toss to coat on all sides. Dust the beef with the jalapeño seasoning rub and mix thoroughly again until the meat is evenly coated. Dry brine in a chamber vacuum sealer to save time or just cover and let sit for 30 minutes.

2. Prepare the smoker with the wood of your choice and heat to medium-high (275°F to 300°F, or 140°C to 150°C). Spray a cast-iron skillet with cooking spray and place it on the smoker's grate. Sear the meat all over for about 3 minutes each side. Transfer to a plate and set aside.

3. Add the garlic to the skillet and stir to coat with the meat drippings. Add the butter and cook until the garlic is browned.

4. Return the meat to the skillet and stir to completely coat it with that garlicky goodness. Sprinkle with the salt and parsley. Cook for 2 minutes more. Transfer the beef to a plate, drizzle with the pan sauce, and serve hot.

SMOKED CAJUN QUESO

YIELD: 10 to 12 servings — PREP: 15 minutes — COOK: 40 minutes

There are dips, and then there are Dips. This is the cheese dip to end all cheese dips, and it is perfect for a large-crowd spread. It will be right at home at a basic backyard party, family get-together, or huge tailgate fan fest. The mix of cheeses are dominated by my particular Cajun-flavored favorite, which essentially stands on top of the base created by the other cheeses. Add in some sausage, shrimp, and specialty spices, and you have a full-bodied dip that eats a lot like a main course. Even though it's a perfect partner to chips of all kinds, it can also be a game-changer as a topping on simple grilled chicken breasts or pork loin.

1 package (12 ounces, or 340 g) andouille sausage

2 packages (8 ounces, or 225 g each) American cheese (I use Velveeta.)

1 package (4 ounces, or 115 g) spiced cheese (I use Big John's Cajun Beehive Cheese.)

1 package (8 ounces, or 225 g) cream cheese

½ cup (120 ml) heavy cream

1 jalapeño, minced

1 can (4 ounces, or 115 g) tiny shrimp

1 tablespoon (10 g) no-salt seasoning blend (I use Tony Chachere's No Salt Seasoning.)

1 teaspoon spicy BBQ rub (I use Blazing Star Reaper Rub and Seasoning.)

1 jalapeño, sliced (for garnish)

Chips of choice

1. Prepare the grill with your favorite briquettes piled to one side and preheat to medium-high (about 350°F, or 180°C).

2. Chop the sausage into 1-inch (2.5 cm) pieces. Cut the Velveeta and Cajun cheeses into quarters (leave the cream cheese brick whole). In a large aluminum roasting pan, combine the cheeses, sausage, and heavy cream. Place the pan on the grill over indirect heat.

3. After about 1 hour, add the jalapeño, shrimp, seasoning blend, and BBQ rub. Mix thoroughly and smoke for 20 minutes more. Top with the jalapeño slices and enjoy with chips of choice!

CHORIZO JALAPEÑO POPPERS

YIELD: 12 poppers — PREP: 40 minutes — COOK: 90 minutes

You may think you've had jalapeño poppers before, and you may even think you've had great jalapeño poppers, but you haven't had the king of poppers until you have them stuffed with chorizo. The combo of flavors in this version is pure money—interesting and one-of-a-kind. I like these with chorizo because it's a smoother texture of sausage with a ton of flavor, and it works perfectly with the creamy blend of cheeses. Adding ranch seasoning might seem like a small thing, or even a little odd, but it puts these poppers over the top. Full warning: One bite of these and you're going to have a tough time stopping yourself from eating all of them. Make extra, just in case.

8 ounces (225 g) chorizo, removed from the casings

1 package (8 ounces, or 225 g) cream cheese

1 package (8 ounces, or 225 g) shredded Mexican-style cheese blend

1 tablespoon (12 g) ranch seasoning, divided (I strongly recommend Woodfire + Whisky Jalapeño Ranch Seasoning.)

6 jalapeños, halved lengthwise and seeded (seeds reserved)

1 package (16 ounces, or 455 g) thin-cut bacon slices (12 slices)

¼ cup (60 g) crema Mexicana

1. In a nonstick pan over medium-high heat, pan-fry the chorizo for 10 minutes or until the internal temperature reaches 165°F (74°C). Drain the grease and transfer the sausage to a large bowl.

2. Add the cream cheese and shredded cheese to the bowl. Mix well. Sprinkle with about two-thirds of the ranch seasoning and the reserved jalapeño seeds. Mash all the ingredients together until you've got a uniform paste texture.

3. Fill each jalapeño half with the chorizo mixture. Wrap each half, all the way around top to bottom, with a slice of thin-cut bacon. Season with a dusting of the ranch seasoning.

4. Prepare the grill with your favorite briquettes, preheated to medium-high or about 350°F (180°C). Grill the poppers for 60 to 70 minutes or until the bacon is crispy but not burned.

5. Drizzle the poppers with the crema Mexicana and serve.

SCORPION CHEESE CRACKERS

YIELD: 2 servings — PREP: 10 minutes — COOK: 60 minutes

I like to reimagine my favorite foods and take them to the next level. That was hard to do with cheese crackers because they are so satisfying and addictive all on their own. But it turns out that all you need is a little duck fat and some scorching hot rub (that I call a "Scorpion" blend) to do the trick. The great thing about duck fat is that it's so rich it can cut through just about any spice blend. But it also coats the taste buds, spreading around any flavors it happens to be carrying. You'll be surprised at just how much a little time in the smoker can change a simple snack food.

2 cups (124 g) cheese crackers (I use Cheez-Its.)

2 tablespoons (28 ml) duck fat

2 tablespoons (24 g) extra spicy BBQ rub (I use Blazing Star BBQ Scorpion Rub and Seasoning.)

1. In a large bowl, drizzle the cheese crackers with the duck fat and toss to coat. Sprinkle with the rub and toss again until the crackers are completely covered on both sides.

2. Prepare the smoker with applewood and heat to about 225°F (107°C).

3. Transfer the crackers to a sheet pan or baking sheet and smoke them for 1 hour or until the coating is very crispy.

PROSCIUTTO-WRAPPED BRIE POPPERS

YIELD: 10 poppers — PREP: 15 minutes — COOK: 1 hour

When I reimagine a bar-snack favorite, I like to really reimagine it. I use Brie in this version of poppers because it melts super creamy and offers a richer, edgier flavor with a little tang to it. Thanks to the thinness of the slices, the crispy prosciutto creates a subtle, salty shell that does the popper proud. This is perfect for any cookout table, but is easy enough to whip up for a weeknight snack or dinner party appetizer (or make a whole meal out of them!).

10 large jalapeño peppers

1 wheel Brie (8 ounces, or 225 g)

¼ cup (72 g) habanero bacon jam

10 slices prosciutto

2 tablespoons (28 ml) olive oil

2 tablespoons (24 g) pork rub-and-seasoning (I recommend Blazing Star Pork'n Rub and Seasoning.)

1. Prepare the smoker with the wood of your choice, heated to medium (about 300°F, or 150°C).

2. Slice each jalapeño in half lengthwise and remove the seeds and veins. Cut the Brie into slices the same size as the split jalapeños. Stuff the cheese into one half of each split jalapeño.

3. Fill the remaining jalapeño halves with the jam. Squeeze the halves together to re-form into complete peppers and roll each one up in a slice of prosciutto.

4. Rub the poppers with olive oil and dust them all around with the pork rub-and-seasoning. Smoke them for about 1 hour or until the prosciutto is crusty. Let rest for 2 to 5 minutes before serving (the cheese will be scalding hot if you don't rest them).

SMOKED CHILI

YIELD: 6 servings — PREP: 30 minutes — COOK: 1 hour

The basic recipe for this chili was already a crowd-pleaser. It combines an amazing blend of spices that are as flavorful as they are fiery. A healthy amount of Mexican beer helps make this a unique and unusual dish, but smoking the roast that is one of two meats in the chili just puts a completely new and wonderful spin on an old classic. Coating the roast in Worcestershire sauce before smoking is the key; it creates a little bit of a salty crust on the meat, which holds strong even as the chili cooks.

1 beef chuck roast (2 pounds, or 910 g)

2 tablespoons (28 ml) Worcestershire sauce

2 tablespoons (28 ml) olive oil

2 pounds (910 g) ground beef

1 yellow onion, peeled and diced

1 bottle (12 ounces, or 355 ml) your favorite Mexican beer

1 can (10 ounces, or 285 g) diced tomatoes and green chilies

1 can (8 ounces, or 225 g) tomato sauce

8 cloves garlic, peeled and minced

1 can (15½ ounces, or 440 g) kidney beans

½ tablespoon ground cumin

1 tablespoon (8 g) chili powder

½ teaspoon ground cayenne pepper

1–2 tablespoons (12–24 g) spicy BBQ rub (I use Blazing Star Reaper Rub and Seasoning.)

1 tablespoon (18 g) salt

1 tablespoon (6 g) coarse ground black pepper

2 teaspoons cornmeal, if needed

2 jalapeños, sliced (for garnish)

Shredded cheese (optional)

1. Prepare the smoker with hickory wood, heated to about 300°F (150°C).

2. Coat the chuck roast all over with the Worcestershire sauce. Smoke it for 2½ hours or until a dark brown crust forms. Remove and let rest for 1 hour.

3. Cut the chuck roast into small chunks, trimming out all connective tissue and fat.

4. In a large pot over medium heat, heat the olive oil. Add the ground beef, breaking it up. Once browned, drain and set aside.

5. Add the onions to the pot and cook until translucent. Return the ground beef to the pot along with the chuck roast. Add the remaining ingredients except for the cornmeal, jalapeños, and cheese. Stir to thoroughly combine the ingredients. Reduce the heat and simmer the chili for 1 hour.

6. Stir in the cornmeal to thicken as necessary. Cook for about 10 minutes more. Serve hot, topped with sliced jalapeños and your favorite shredded cheese, if desired.

HAWAIIAN-STYLE KALUA PORK SLIDERS

YIELD: 10 to 12 servings — PREP: 30 minutes — COOK: 8½ hours

Every island culture has its own way of doing things, and every so often I look for influences beyond the Philippines. This one comes from the land of whole pigs cooked over open pits, so it has its own honest BBQ lineage. Smoking pork low and slow wrapped in banana leaves (available at most well-stocked Asian markets) gives the sliders that kind of smoke-drenched, fall-apart-tender meat that home Pitmasters dream about. Although you can slather the meat in your favorite BBQ sauce, I'd recommend you use the Hawaiian sauce I specify in the ingredients list. Coupled with sea salt native to the big island, it creates a flavor that you won't find anywhere else.

6–8 large banana leaves

1 pork shoulder or butt (4–6 pounds, or 1.8–2.7 kg)

1 tablespoon (15 ml) hickory or mesquite liquid smoke

2–3 teaspoons (8–12 g) red Hawaiian sea salt

2–3 cups (180–270 g) coarsely chopped cabbage

10–12 Hawaiian sweet slider buns (I use King's Hawaiian Original Hawaiian Sweet Rolls.)

½ cup (152 g) Hawaiian BBQ sauce (I recommend King's Hawaiian Original Sweet Pineapple BBQ Sauce.)

1. Prepare the smoker with hickory wood, heated to low heat or about 225°F (107°C).

2. Moisten the banana leaves and lay them out on a work surface. Overlap the leaves to create a single sheet. Place the pork in the center of the leaves and pat it dry. Pierce it all over with a fork. Coat the meat evenly with the liquid smoke and sprinkle liberally with the sea salt.

3. Wrap the meat up in the banana leaves and place in a large roasting pan. Transfer the pan to the smoker and smoke for 6 to 8 hours or until the meat's internal temperature reaches 205°F (96°C).

4. Let the meat rest for 1 hour. Pour the liquid out of the roasting pan into a large bowl.

5. Pull apart and shred the pork by hand. Mix in the chopped cabbage. Add the reserved liquid and massage it into the mixture. Return the mixture back into the pan and smoke for 30 minutes or until the cabbage is softened.

6. Coat the bottom of each slider bun with the BBQ sauce. Mound the pork mixture on the bottom and then top with top half of the bun. Serve and enjoy!

GARLIC BREAD

YIELD: 4 to 6 servings — PREP: 30 minutes — COOK: 75 minutes

Smoked garlic bread? You bet. You might think that garlic bread toasted in an oven is good enough, but one bite of this delectable side dish is going to change your mind. Both the garlic and the bread itself are smoked in this recipe, so you're getting a full dose of that deep, rich caramelization and wood-smoke goodness. The bread naturally absorbs the complex flavor of the wood, and the smoke fuses the cheese and topping to the loaf. I add this to almost all my friend-and-family cookouts and any party food spread. But it can also add an unusual and interesting twist on a classic element of a traditional Italian dinner.

2 heads garlic, peeled and minced

2 tablespoons (28 ml) olive oil

Salt and pepper to taste

2 sticks (8 ounces, or 225 g) unsalted butter, room temperature

½ cup (30 g) chopped fresh parsley

1 tablespoon (8 g) coarse ground black pepper

1 tablespoon (7 g) smoked paprika

½ cup (40 g) shredded Parmesan cheese

1 loaf French bread, cut in half lengthwise

1. Prepare the smoker with applewood, heated to 250°F (120°C).

2. Cut the tops off of the garlic heads. Drizzle the exposed cloves with olive oil. Dust them with salt and pepper. Wrap them in the aluminum foil and smoke for 1 hour.

3. Remove the garlic and squeeze the roasted cloves out into a large bowl. Add the butter, parsley, pepper, paprika, and Parmesan. Mash together with a fork or wooden spoon until completely integrated. Spread the mixture evenly across the faces of the two French bread halves.

4. Increase the smoker temperature to about 300°F (150°C). Smoke the bread for 10 to 15 minutes or until the butter and cheese are entirely melted. Cut into generous slices and enjoy!

SMOKED PROSCIUTTO CREAM CHEESE

YIELD: 4 to 6 servings — PREP: 10 minutes — COOK: 1 hour

Smoking is the perfect way to crisp up prosciutto, and crunchy prosciutto is absolutely the ideal complement to silky smooth cream cheese, especially when the cheese has done its time in the smoke. It may look like there's not much to this dish—and it is simple—but don't be deceived: The end result is much greater than the sum of its basic parts. Make this alongside other smoked items, and it won't take much effort at all, but it will pay off with a jackpot of flavor in perfect partnership with rich velvety and crunchy textures.

1 package (8 ounces, or 225 g) cream cheese

¼ cup (48 g) spicy BBQ rub (I use Blazing Star Reaper Rub and Seasoning.)

3 slices (3 ounces, or 85 g) prosciutto, diced

2 tablespoons (28 ml) truffle oil

Crackers, bread, or chips of choice

1. Prepare the smoker with applewood, heated to about 225°F (107°F).

2. Unwrap the cream cheese and score it deeply in a grid pattern of small squares on both sides. Coat the cheese all over with the rub, patting to help the spices adhere. Top with a generous layer of the diced prosciutto.

3. Coat a cast-iron pan with the truffle oil. Transfer the cream cheese to the pan and then put the pan in the smoker. Smoke for 1 hour or until the prosciutto is crispy. Serve immediately with crackers, bread, or chips.

SMOKED HAMBURGER HELPER

YIELD: 4 servings — PREP: 5 minutes — COOK: 25 minutes

If you grew up with Hamburger Helper as the dish that stretched the last of your family's meat until payday, welcome to the new elevated version. This one incorporates its own pasta base—a corkscrew macaroni that provides maximum surface area to capture every last bit of the flavor-packed sauce and spices. I'd strongly recommend you use ground Wagyu rather than plain ground beef; it will do the dish proud and add one more layer of complex flavors and richness. Although there are a lot of ingredients, don't be fooled—you can pretty much whip this up at the last minute on a busy weeknight.

1 tablespoon (15 ml) olive oil

1 pound (455 g) ground beef (I recommend ground Wagyu.)

1 tablespoon (8 g) cornstarch

1 tablespoon (7 g) smoked paprika

1½ teaspoons garlic powder

1½ teaspoons onion powder

1½ teaspoons kosher salt

1 teaspoon granulated sugar

½ teaspoon coarse ground black pepper

1 tablespoon (12 g) BBQ seasoning

1 tablespoon (10 g) minced garlic

2 cups (475 ml) beef broth

1½ cups (355 ml) whole milk

2 cups (150 g) uncooked cavatappi pasta (or substitute elbow macaroni [224 g])

2 cups (240 g) grated cheddar cheese

Hot sauce, to taste (optional)

Crispy fried garlic (optional)

1. Prepare a smoker with hickory wood, heated to about 450°F (230°F).

2. In a large cast-iron skillet over medium-high heat, heat the olive oil. Add the ground beef and break it up with a wooden spoon. Cook until browned.

3. Add the cornstarch, spices, and minced garlic and mix well. Cook for 2 minutes and then add the broth, milk, and pasta. Stir to mix well and bring to a boil. Transfer the skillet to the smoker. Smoke the mixture for 10 minutes, stirring halfway through.

4. Remove the skillet and top with the cheddar cheese. Stir until incorporated. Add a couple dashes of hot sauce, if preferred, and garnish with crispy fried garlic if desired. Serve hot.

SHRIMP SURF-AND-TURF TACOS

YIELD: 2 servings — PREP: 30 minutes — COOK: 40 minutes

I'll let you in on a little Pitmaster secret: Combine sweet, delectable shrimp and some of the best meat you can buy, and you don't need a lot of bells and whistles. That's the idea behind this incredible meal-in-one that hits all the high notes. The natural flavors speak for themselves, which is why I didn't go wild with extra flavors. A dusting of beef rub and a hint of garlic are really plenty to round out the dish and let the meat and seafood shine through. It also means that the dish is easy and quick to create, making it an anytime meal that will please the entire family.

½ cup (120 ml) olive oil, divided

3 tablespoons (30 g) no-salt Cajun seasoning

1 tablespoon (14 g) garlic paste

½ pound (225 g) jumbo shrimp, shelled and deveined

1 pound (455 g) American Wagyu steak tips

3 tablespoons (36 g) beef rub (I use Blazing Star Beef Rub and Seasoning.)

2 corn tortillas

½ cup (2 ounces, or 57 g) shredded Oaxaca cheese

2 tablespoons (30 g) crema Mexicana

1 tablespoon (1 g) chopped cilantro

1. In a small bowl, combine ¼ cup (60 ml) of the olive oil, the Cajun seasoning, and the garlic paste. Mix well until completely combined.

2. Add the shrimp and toss until well coated. Cover and refrigerate for 1 hour or place in a chamber vacuum sealer set to the marinate function (run it two to three times, for maximum marinade saturation).

3. Cut the steak tips into small strips. In a large bowl, coat the meat in the remaining olive oil and season with the beef rub.

4. Heat the griddle on high. Cook the meat to medium-rare, about 3 minutes on each side or to an internal temperature of 135°F (57°C). Transfer to a plate and set aside.

5. Cook the shrimp on the griddle for about 1 minute on each side or until they turn pink and begin to curl. Set aside.

6. Lay the tortillas on the griddle and top with a layer of the cheese. Heat the tortillas until the cheese melts entirely.

7. Line the steak tips along the center of each tortilla and lay three to four shrimp on top. Drizzle with the crema Mexicana and sprinkle with the cilantro. Roll up and enjoy!

GRILLED MOLLEJAS
(AKA SWEETBREADS)

YIELD: 2 servings — PREP: 5 minutes — COOK: 90 minutes

Yes, mollejas are a variety meat—specifically, veal thymus glands. The thing about organ meats is that they are usually remarkably flavorful, and mollejas are at the top of hill when it comes a delicate, sweet richness. They are so delicious that I don't do much more than a light seasoning when I grill them. I like to let the flavor shine through. They are also fantastically tender and pure pleasure to eat as long as you aren't bothered by where in the animal they come from.

1 pound (455 g) mollejas (I get mine from Wild Fork Foods.)

1 tablespoon (12 g) grilling salt (I use Al Frugoni Grilling Salt.)

1 lemon, halved

1. Prepare the grill for direct heat over a steady medium heat, about 300°F (150°C).

2. Pat the mollejas dry and season with the salt.

3. Grill the meat for about 1 hour or until the outside is crispy. Flip frequently to avoid burning. Don't worry if you leave the meat on the grill too long; it's almost impossible to overcook these. Place the lemon halves face down on the grill.

4. About halfway through cooking, spritz the meat with one of the lemon halves. When the meat is cooked, transfer to a serving plate, cut into 1-inch (2.5 cm) slices, and squeeze the second lemon half over the meat before serving.

PULLED LAMB TOSTADAS

YIELD: 10 to 12 servings — PREP: 40 minutes — COOK: 6 hours

There's a reason that Middle Eastern cultures have, for so long, embraced lamb as a meat of choice. It is ideal for slow, natural cooking—the longer, the better. As it cooks, the fat in the perfectly marbled meat renders down and naturally moisturizes the cut. That creates even more tenderness in a meat that is already mind-blowingly tender. Longer cooking times also guarantee that any connective tissues are broken down so that you wind up with an absolute pleasure to eat. Really, all lamb needs in the way of seasoning is some salty condiments to be absolutely delectable. Word to the wise: I get my lamb from a butcher to ensure that it's as fresh as possible, and I'd suggest you do too.

For the Lamb

1 lamb shoulder (3–4 pounds, or 1.4–1.8 kg)

½ cup plus 2 tablespoons (148 ml) Worcestershire sauce, divided (I use Bear & Burton's Fireshire.)

2 tablespoons (24 g) garlic jalapeño rub (I use Kosmos Q The Best Garlic Jalapeno Rub.)

2 cups (475 ml) beef broth

2 large carrots, chopped

6 cloves garlic, peeled

For the Chimichurri

1 small shallot, peeled and chopped

1 head garlic, peeled and chopped

1 bunch parsley, coarsely chopped

1 bunch cilantro, coarsely chopped

2 habanero peppers, chopped

¼ cup (60 ml) red wine vinegar

½ cup (120 ml) roasted almond oil (I use Fresh Vintage Farms.)

1 teaspoon applewood smoked salt (I use Osmo Applewood Smoked Sea Salt.)

10–12 small corn tortillas

1. Prepare the smoker with cherrywood, heated to about 275°F (140°C).

2. Coat the lamb in the ½ cup (120 ml) Worcestershire and then dust all over with jalapeño rub. Smoke the meat for 4 to 5 hours or until the internal temperature reaches 180°F (82°C).

3. In a large roasting pan, combine the broth and 2 tablespoons (28 ml) Worcestershire sauce and mix. Transfer the lamb shoulder to the pan. Add in the carrots and garlic and place the pan in the smoker until the internal temperature reaches 200°F (93°C).

4. Combine all the chimichurri ingredients in a large bowl and mix thoroughly.

5. Let the smoked lamb rest for 45 to 60 minutes. Pull it apart and shred it with your hands or use a fork.

6. Pile a generous mound of lamb in the middle of a tortilla. Cover with a heaping spoonful of the chimichurri and serve.

LONGANISA BREAKFAST SMASHBURGER

YIELD: 4 servings —— PREP: 10 minutes —— COOK: 15 minutes

Longanisa is the sausage of choice in the Philippines and for good reason. It's a unique blend of flavors that brings to mind chorizo, only a little sweeter and more complex. Filipinos use it in many ways (because the flavor never grows old), but one of the most popular is to make it the centerpiece of a breakfast sandwich—which is usually closer to a breakfast burger. I took my inspiration in this recipe from that idea, which is why I've included an egg and bacon. That said, there's no reason to limit this fabulously filling meal to a morning wake-up call. It's just as good as an easy dinner treat and will fit right in at your next cookout.

2 pounds (910 g) longanisa sausage

½ cup (120 g) pork panko (ground pork rinds)

1 tablespoon (12 g) spicy BBQ rub, plus more as needed (I use Blazing Star Reaper Rub and Seasoning.)

5 large eggs, divided

8 strips bacon

4 slices pepper Jack cheese

4 hamburger buns

2 tablespoons (28 g) mayonnaise

1. Remove the sausage from the casings. In a large bowl, combine the meat, pork panko, BBQ rub, and 1 egg. Mash together using your hands until completely combined. Form into four equal balls.

2. On a griddle over high heat, cook the remaining 4 eggs over easy and cook the bacon until crispy.

3. While the eggs and bacon cook, place the four sausage balls onto the griddle. Use a weight to smash them into flat patties. Dust with more BBQ rub and cook for about 3 minutes before flipping. The sausage should be slightly charred. Top each patty with a slice of cheese and cook for 3 minutes more.

4. Toast each hamburger bun half face down on the griddle for 1 minute. Assemble each patty starting with the bottom of a bun. Smear about ½ tablespoon of mayonnaise on the bottom and top with a burger. Place a cooked egg on the burger and then cover with the bacon strips and the bun top. Repeat with the remaining ingredients and enjoy.

BIGGER, BETTER FAST FOOD BURGER

YIELD: 1 serving — PREP: 5 minutes — COOK: 20 minutes

I grew up loving me some Mickey D's, especially the classic Big Mac. It's such a great grab-and-go meal in your hand that I wanted to put my own spin on it. That's how I came to create this even bigger, better, and spicier version. The sauce is key, and I spent a lot of time experimenting with spice blends to come up with truly memorable combination of flavors that both stands on its own and does the meat justice. Speaking of the meat, if you're going to reinvent a classic, you better bring the good stuff. That's why I chose to cook up Angus patties for this sandwich. Buy the best you can find and make that burger big enough to impress—mine are a full half pound (225 g) of juicy, salty, spicy goodness.

For the Spicy Better Big Mac Sauce

½ cup (115 g) mayonnaise

2 tablespoons (30 g) dill pickle relish

1 tablespoon (14 g) garlic paste

2 tablespoons (35 g) spicy BBQ sauce of choice

2 teaspoons yellow mustard

1 teaspoon white vinegar

1 teaspoon granulated sugar

½ teaspoon smoked paprika

¼ teaspoon kosher salt

¼ teaspoon garlic powder

¼ teaspoon onion powder

¼ teaspoon ground cayenne pepper

For the Burger

2 prepared extra-large Angus beef patties (8 ounces, or 225 g each) or substitute (I use Meat District THE SHAQ Premium Burger Patties.)

2 tablespoons (24 g) beef rub (I use Blazing Star Beef Rub and Seasoning.)

2 slices American cheese

2 sesame seed hamburger buns

¼ cup (18 g) shredded lettuce

4 pickle slices

1. Prepare the grill with premium charcoal, heated to medium-high or about 350°F (180°C).

2. In a small bowl, combine all the sauce ingredients. Mix well and set aside.

3. Season the beef patties with the beef rub. Grill for 3 minutes before flipping. Top each patty with a slice of cheese and close the grill lid. Grill until the burgers reach an internal temperature of 135°F (57°C).

4. Toast the buns (including a second bottom for the center of the burger).

5. Smear a bun bottom with the sauce and top with the lettuce. Place a patty on this bed, smear it with a dollop of sauce, and top with second bun bottom. Spread sauce on the second bottom, a layer of pickles, the second patty, and then the bun top. Eat it while it's hot!

THE CHRISTMAS BURGER

YIELD: 1 serving — PREP: 10 minutes — COOK: 10 minutes

Here's a happy yuletide present that you shouldn't put under the tree. This unusual burger is a quick-grilling dream to eat and features the distinctive tart holiday flavor of cranberries. I used cranberry sauce to cut through some of the richer ingredients, and the combination is a rock star meal that you'll want to go to again and again, even long after the holidays are over. It's not just about the flavors, either. Thanks to ultra-crispy pancetta, crumbly blue cheese, and a small serving of crispy fresh greens, there are plenty of textures to keep your mouth interested while you fill your belly. Make it for yourself whenever the hunger hits you; it's a gift that doesn't need to be wrapped.

For the Blue Cheese Dressing

1 tablespoon (14 g) mayonnaise

1½ tablespoons (23 g) sour cream

½ cup (60 g) blue cheese crumbles

Juice ½ lemon

Pinch salt and freshly cracked pepper

Pinch granulated garlic

For the Burger

1 prepared extra-large Angus beef patty (8 ounces, or 225 g) (I use Meat District THE SHAQ Premium Burger Patty.)

1 tablespoon (12 g) BBQ rub of choice

2–4 slices thin-sliced pancetta

1 brioche bun

1 tablespoon (14 g) cranberry sauce

1 tablespoon (2 g) microgreens

1. Prepare the grill with premium charcoal, heated to medium-high or about 350°F (180°C).

2. In a small bowl, combine all the dressing ingredients. Mix well with a fork and set aside.

3. Season the burger on both sides with the BBQ rub. Grease a sheet pan with cooking spray and arrange the pancetta slices on the pan. Transfer the burger and pan to the grill.

4. Grill the burger for 3 minutes each side or until the internal temperature reaches 135°F (57°C). Cook the pancetta until crispy.

5. Toast the bun. Smear the bottom with cranberry sauce and layer the burger, the pancetta, a healthy dollop of blue cheese dressing, the microgreens, and the top of the bun. Enjoy!

BUFFALO SHRIMP ON STEROIDS

YIELD: 4 servings — PREP: 10 minutes — COOK: 20 minutes

What I mean by "steroids" in a recipe like this is that I've dialed the flavors up to eleven. I start with the rich, sweet flesh of shrimp and just build from there. That sweetness is the perfect foil and stage for an off-the-hook spice blend that brings the heat for days. I bread the shrimp in pork panko. Regular panko is just finely ground bread crumbs. Pork panko is crumbled pork rinds, which gives the breading a satisfyingly smooth, silky texture. Add in a few surprise ingredients like the everything bagel seasoning, and you wind up with a truly memorable dish that you'll be thinking about long after you've finished it.

For the Shrimp

3 large eggs

¼ cup (31 g) all-purpose flour

1 cup (240 g) pork panko (ground pork rinds)

2 pounds (910 g) medium shrimp, shelled and deveined

2 cups (475 ml) peanut oil

1 tablespoon (18 g) sea salt

For the TFTI Buffalo BBQ Sauce

¼ cup (60 ml) almond oil

1 tablespoon (14 g) minced garlic

1 tablespoon (4 g) crushed chili flakes

1 tablespoon (12 g) everything bagel seasoning

2 tablespoons (32 g) BBQ sauce (I use Blazing Star Original BBQ Sauce.)

1 cup (240 g) buffalo sauce (I use Tacticalories HELLDIVER Buffalo Wing Sauce.)

1 tablespoon (12 g) spicy BBQ rub (I use Blazing Star Reaper Rub and Seasoning.)

4 tablespoons (55 g) salted butter

1. In a large shallow bowl, whisk the eggs until uniform and then whisk in the flour. Place the pork panko in a separate shallow bowl.

2. Dunk the shrimp in the egg-and-flour mixture until coated all over. Press into the panko until completely breaded.

3. In a deep cast-iron skillet or pot, heat the oil to about 350°F (180°C). Fry the shrimp in small batches, 2 to 3 minutes on each side or until golden brown. Sprinkle with sea salt.

4. In a small cast-iron pot, heat the almond oil over medium-high heat. Add the garlic and cook for 2 minutes. Add the remaining sauce ingredients and stir to combine. Simmer until the sauce thickens slightly, about 5 minutes.

5. Transfer the shrimp to a serving platter, drizzle with the sauce, and enjoy.

SMOKE IT

When I first started off smoking BBQ, I used a traditional wood-fired offset smoker like I saw on all the YouTube videos and barbecue shows that I watched. I loved the idea of low-and-slow cooking (low temperatures paired with exceptionally long cook times). It seemed to be the way to go for authentic smoky flavor and true BBQ. Smoking with an offset rig turned out to be more of a challenge than I had bargained for, though, and led to a lot of failed food experiments.

I eventually switched to a pellet smoker. These smokers are much easier to use. Basically, you fill the smoke chamber with a load of compressed wood pellets, dial in the temperature, and the unit does the rest. They are pretty much "set-it-and-forget-it" simple.

The experience gave me a chance to learn how smoke behaves, how it works with different proteins, and how temperatures should be maintained throughout the smoking process. I eventually found my way back to an offset smoker once I had the knowledge and experience to use it successfully. Personally, I find the flavor of pure wood-smoked proteins superior to pellet-smoked food. Full disclosure: A lot of people disagree with me on that, so you should judge for yourself.

No matter what type of smoker you're working with, start with the traditional smoke flavor sponges. That means pork, like the BBQ Whiskey Pork Spare Ribs on page 180, and sturdy cuts of beef, like the picanha in the Picanha and Habanero Chimichurri Sandwich on page 197. Tri-tip, ribs, and brisket are all classic smoked meats, too.

Once you get comfortable with the process and hone your chops, you can branch out and start smoking fish and even whole chickens or turkeys. Whatever you put into the smoker, you're going to enjoy a flavor and surface texture unlike those from any other cooking method. There is no matching the deep, rich, fruity, sweet goodness that wood smoke gives to everything it touches. And you can change the flavor as you prefer, simply by using a different wood.

BACON-WRAPPED PORK BELLY LOLLIPOPS

YIELD: 4 servings — PREP: 30 minutes — COOK: 4 hours

With all due respect to candy stores, this is by far and away my favorite type of lollipop. If you love pork as much as I do, I bet it'll be your favorite too. Wrapping pork belly in bacon pretty much guarantees juiciness no matter how long you smoke these. The BBQ rub and sauce are there to cut some of the richness of the lollipop, but you can try your own spices or favorite pork seasonings. These really are flavor canvases that could be modified in many different ways to suit individual tastes and preferences.

1 pound (455 g) pork belly strips

2 tablespoons (24 g) BBQ rub
(I use RubCity Smoke Mafia.)

8 slices bacon

⅓ cup (85 g) BBQ sauce

1 tablespoon (20 g) honey

Bacon crumbles (optional)

1. Prepare the smoker with applewood, heated to about 250°F (120°C).

2. Cut the pork belly strips in half. Skewer each half through the end. Dust each side of each strip with BBQ rub.

3. Wrap the lollipops tightly using 2 slices of bacon for each lollipop. Secure the bacon with toothpicks as necessary. Dust both sides with more BBQ rub.

4. Smoke the lollipops for 3 to 4 hours or until they are tender when probed. Coat the lollipops all over with BBQ sauce. Continue smoking for 20 minutes more or until the sauce has crusted on the surface.

5. Drizzle the hot lollipops with honey and bacon crumbles, if desired. Serve with plenty of napkins!

THE PORK TRIFECTA

YIELD: 6 to 8 servings — PREP: 40 minutes — COOK: 2½ hours

Pork lovers, here you go. If this isn't enough of the pig for you, then you'll never get enough pig. This mix of meats never fails to satisfy even the most robust appetite by combining the unique sweet spice blend of chorizo with the understated flavor of pork loins and the absolute fatty perfection of strip bacon. Add a little bit of cheese and a superstar pork rub and you have the makings of a truly magical meal. Just make sure you let it rest for the full recommended time, so that the flavors can saturate the meat.

1 pound (455 g) ground chorizo

2 pork loins (1½ pounds, or 680 g each)

2 packages (8 ounces, or 225 g) Mexican-style shredded cheese blend

2 packages (12 ounces, or 340 g) bacon

¼ cup (48 g) BBQ pork rub (I use Blazing Star Pork'n Rub and Seasoning.)

1. Prepare the smoker with applewood, heated to about 250°F (120°C).

2. In a large skillet over medium-high heat, cook the chorizo until the oil separates from the meat. Drain the oil and set the meat aside.

3. Trim the fat and membrane from the pork loins. Butterfly each pork loin (cutting lengthwise, but not all the way through, so that the pork loin can be splayed open). Wrap them in butcher or food-grade kraft paper and smash with a rolling pin until they are about half their original thickness.

4. Smear equal amounts of chorizo on each pork loin. Top with the shredded cheese. Roll up each pork loin tightly along the length to create a log.

5. Seal each loin end with two strips of bacon and then wrap the entire loin in bacon, with the strips wrapped around the loin. Season all around with the pork rub. Pat the loins to ensure the rub sticks to the bacon.

6. Smoke the loins for 2 hours or until the internal temperature reaches 120°F (49°C). Increase the smoker temperature to 300°F (150°C) and continue smoking the loins for 30 to 45 minutes or until the internal temperature reaches 145°F (63°C) and the bacon is crispy.

7. Let the loins rest for about 20 minutes before cutting into 1 inch (2.5 cm)-thick slices and serving.

PASTRAMI BEEF RIBS

YIELD: 6 to 8 servings — PREP: 30 minutes — BRINING: 5 to 7 days — COOK: 9 to 12 hours

If you're a fan of the sliced deli meat, wait till you try pastrami ribs. The brine and rub in this recipe focus on that familiar salt-forward flavor. But the smoking is the key. A slow smoke makes for the type of tenderness meat-lovers go crazy for, and it intensifies the peppery notes as well as boosting all the flavors. Take note that you'll need to order dino (dinosaur) short ribs, a type taken from the shoulder. Dino short ribs are exceptionally flavorful and essential to this recipe. Don't be surprised if these become your go-to ribs, like they have for me.

For the Brine

1½ gallons (5.6 L) water

3 cups (672 g) kosher salt

1½ cups (300 g) granulated sugar

2 tablespoons (38 g) pink curing salt

1 clove garlic, peeled

¼ cup (25 g) pickling spice

4 to 5 pounds (1.8 to 2.3 kg) ice

4 to 6 pounds (1.8 to 2.7 kg) dino short ribs

For the Rub

2 tablespoons (10 g) black peppercorns

2 tablespoons (10 g) coriander seeds

1 tablespoon (11 g) mustard seeds

1 tablespoon (14 g) kosher salt

2 tablespoons (14 g) smoked paprika

1 tablespoon (9 g) garlic powder

2 tablespoons (30 g) dark brown sugar

1 tablespoon (8 g) chili powder (optional)

½ cup (120 g) Dijon mustard

1. In a large pot over high heat, bring the water for the brine to a boil. Add the other brine ingredients and boil, stirring constantly, until the salts and sugar completely dissolve.

2. Fill a large bucket with the ice and pour in the brine. Trim the ribs and transfer to the brine. Refrigerate for 5 to 7 days.

3. When you're ready to cook the ribs, prep the smoker with your favorite wood, heated to about 250°F (120°C). Combine the peppercorns, coriander seeds, and mustard seeds in a pan over medium heat. Toast until fragrant.

4. Process the toasted seeds in a spice grinder or a food processor. In a large bowl, combine the ground seeds with the remaining rub ingredients and mix well.

5. Remove the ribs from the brine, rinse, drain, and pat dry. Slather with the mustard and coat with the rub. Smoke the ribs for 8 to 10 hours. Let rest for 1 hour before slicing and serving.

FOIL BOAT–METHOD BRISKET

YIELD: 6 to 8 servings — PREP: 1 hour — COOK: 14 to 24 hours

The foil boat method is a way of smoking ingredients together, wrapped up in one packet that seals in juices and flavor. This recipe uses an adaptation, where a brisket is wrapped in butcher or food-grade kraft paper to finish cooking. The principal is the same: Keep flavor and moisture contained while still infusing the meat with an alluring smoky flavor. You don't need a ton of spices for this one because the meat itself is so naturally flavorful and rich. One note though: The recipe involves saving fat trimmings so that they can be rendered in the smoker and used to bump the flavor of the completely smoked meat. If you have your butcher trim the cut, you'll need to ask him to save the fat. You might also want to set aside some of those trimmings to add to burgers or other beef cuts. It adds a silky richness to any meat.

1 Australian Wagyu brisket
(8–9 pounds, or 3.6–4.1 kg)
(I get mine from High
Society Meats.)

1 cup (235 ml) hot sauce
(I use FYR BLK hot sauce.)

2 cups (320 g) SPG seasoning
(I use Chuds BBQ SPG.)

1. Trim the brisket, removing the thick fat and silver skin. This is easiest if the brisket has been refrigerated for at least an hour (you can even place it in freezer for 20 minutes before trimming to make the job really easy). Save the fat trimmings in a roasting pan and leave behind a thin layer of fat to protect the meat.

2. Coat the brisket all over with the hot sauce. Season liberally with the SPG seasoning.

3. Prepare the smoker with your favorite wood, heated to about 225°F (107°C). You'll add wood for the first 2 to 3 hours of smoking to max out the wood flavor in the meat.

4. Place the brisket in the smoker fat-side up. Place the pan with the fat trimmings in the smoker and close the lid.

(CONTINUED)

5. When the internal temperature of the meat reaches 170°F to 180°F (77°C to 82°C), remove the brisket and place it on a large, double layer of aluminum foil with some of the rendered tallow from the fat trimmings under the meat. Form a basin around the brisket to hold in the juices.

6. Increase the smoker's heat to 250°F (120°C). Pour half of the remaining tallow over the brisket and return it to the smoker. After 2 to 3 hours or when the brisket's internal temperature reaches 195°F to 200°F (91°C to 93°C), check the meat with a probe to judge the tenderness. When the probe goes smoothly into the meat with very little resistance, remove it from the smoker.

7. Preheat the oven to 170°F (77°C). Transfer the brisket to a large sheet of butcher paper. Coat the meat with half the remaining tallow and wrap it up tightly in the paper. Transfer it to a large aluminum roasting pan and pour the remaining tallow over the wrapped brisket.

8. Leave the brisket in the oven until you're ready to slice it—up to 12 hours. The longer the meat rests, the juicier and more tender it will be. When you're ready to serve, remove the brisket and slice it up.

PEANUT CURRY SMOKED PORK RIBS

YIELD: 4 to 6 servings — PREP: 30 minutes — COOK: 3½ hours

This dish includes a couple of curveballs that separates it from more-traditional rib recipes. Most importantly, I use St. Louis–style ribs. They're meatier and fatter than baby back ribs, which translates to a whole lot more flavor when you smoke them right. The cut is taken from the lower portion of the ribs, on the belly. The bones are bigger, but that just means the cut holds moisture a little better. Using St. Louis–style ribs means trimming off the connective tissue and cartilage that holds the ribs to the breastbone. It's not a huge job, but you can always have the butcher do it for you. I also use peanut butter in the curry sauce. I think you're going to be blown away by how naturally the flavor goes with smoked pork—it's a match made in taste bud heaven.

For the Ribs

1 St. Louis–style pork rib slab (3½ pounds, or 1.6 kg)

2 tablespoons (36 g) salt

2 tablespoons (12 g) coarse ground black pepper

For the Rub

2 teaspoons onion powder

1 tablespoon (9 g) garlic powder

1 tablespoon (6 g) ground ginger

1 teaspoon curry powder

1 teaspoon cinnamon

1 teaspoon crushed red pepper flakes

For the Peanut Curry Sauce

½ cup (120 ml) water

¼ cup (60 g) packed light brown sugar

3 tablespoons (45 ml) soy sauce

1 tablespoon (6 g) curry powder

1 teaspoon crushed red pepper flakes

½ cup (130 g) creamy peanut butter

For Serving

1 tablespoon (6 g) chopped fresh chives

2 teaspoons sea salt

(CONTINUED)

1. Prepare the smoker with hickory wood, heated to about 300°F (150°C). (You can cook them in an oven at 300°F [150°C, or gas mark 2] if you don't own a smoker.)

2. With the rib slab bone-side up, remove the membrane by either pulling it off or using a knife to carefully cut it off. Season the ribs on both sides with the salt and pepper.

3. In a large bowl, combine all the ingredients for the dry rub and whisk together. Coat the ribs on both sides with the dry rub.

4. Smoke for 1½ hours uncovered. Remove and wrap the ribs in aluminum foil. Return them to the smoker and smoke for an additional 1½ hours. Remove and let the ribs rest for 30 minutes.

5. While the ribs are resting, make the sauce. In a 4-quart (3.8 L) saucepan over medium-low heat, combine all the sauce ingredients. Whisk constantly until the sauce thickens, about 5 minutes.

6. Slice the ribs and baste liberally on both sides with the sauce. Transfer the individual ribs to a large cast-iron pan and baste with any remaining sauce.

7. Finish the ribs in the smoker for 5 minutes. Sprinkle with the chives and sea salt and serve.

TOMAHAWK STEAK
WITH CAJUN COWBOY BUTTER

YIELD: 4 servings — PREP: 30 minutes — COOK: 90 minutes

This recipe makes the most of my favorite cut of meat. If you've never experienced a tomahawk steak, you haven't really lived. It's taken from the rib section and is one of the best marbled cuts you can get off a steer. The meat is naturally so tender it almost melts on your tongue. It already has an enticing buttery taste, but my Cajun Cowboy Butter takes it just a bit closer to pure heaven. Here's a word of caution though: Don't rush a cut like this. It needs to rest after cooking, and slicing it up too early can mean losing a lot of super tasty juices.

For the Steak

1 tomahawk steak (1½–2 pounds, or 680–910 g)

2 tablespoons (28 ml) olive oil, plus more as needed

3 tablespoons (36 g) Creole seasoning (I use Tony Chachere's BOLD Creole Seasoning.)

For the Cajun Cowboy Butter

2 sticks (8 ounces, or 225 g) unsalted butter

1 head garlic, peeled and minced

1 small shallot, peeled and minced

2 tablespoons (30 g) Dijon mustard

1 teaspoon paprika

Pinch ground cayenne pepper

Juice ½ lemon

1 tablespoon (12 g) spice-and-herb seasoning blend (I use Tony Chachere's Spice N' Herbs Creole Seasoning.)

1 tablespoon (15 ml) Louisiana-style pepper sauce (I use Tony Chachere's Louisiana Pepper Sauce.)

2 teaspoons minced fresh thyme

2 tablespoons (8 g) chopped fresh parsley

1 tablespoon (6 g) chopped fresh chives

1 teaspoon coarse ground black pepper

1. Coat the steak all over with the olive oil. Dust both sides with the Creole seasoning. Drill a hole in the end of the bone and hang the steak over an open fire of lump charcoal and hickory wood.

2. In a cast-iron pan over medium heat, melt the butter. Add the garlic and shallots and cook them until fragrant.

3. Add the mustard, paprika, cayenne pepper, lemon juice, spice-and-herb blend, and pepper sauce. Stir well to incorporate the flavors and then add the thyme, parsley, chives, and pepper. Cook for 1 minute and then transfer to a small bowl.

4. After 30 to 40 minutes or when the steak reaches an internal temperature of 115°F (46°C), remove it and set aside.

5. Place a large cast-iron pan upside down over the coals. (This will allow you to lay the tomahawk flat for an even sear without the bone getting in the way.) Drizzle the pan with olive oil and sear the steak for about 1 to 2 minutes per side or until the internal temperature reaches 130°F (54°C).

6. Let the steak rest for 5 to 10 minutes before slicing. Serve with the Cajun Cowboy Butter and enjoy!

BBQ WHISKEY PORK SPARE RIBS

YIELD: 4 servings — PREP: 40 minutes — COOK: 4 hours

Nothing screams classic BBQ quite like a rack of spare ribs, and nothing goes quite so well on those ribs as a whiskey-based sauce. (Worth mentioning that this sauce will also keep, refrigerated, for up to two weeks and gives a wonderful boost to just about any cut of pork.) Keep in mind that anytime you make this type of sauce or a baste, the whiskey matters. There are so many flavor profiles among different spirits, from the leaner, slightly spicy edge of rye whiskey, to the more traditional, deep, caramel notes in a well-aged bourbon. Experiment with different whiskeys to find new and exciting flavors and don't forget to pour a little for the Pitmaster!

For the Ribs

2 racks spare ribs (2 pounds, or 910 g each)

¼ cup (60 ml) sweet and spicy BBQ sauce (I use Bear & Burtons Breakfast Sauce.)

3 tablespoons (36 g) spicy BBQ rub (I use Blazing Star Reaper Rub and Seasoning.)

For the Whiskey BBQ Sauce

1½ cups (360 g) ketchup

1 cup (235 ml) whiskey (I use Gold Bar Original Whiskey.)

⅓ cup (75 g) packed light brown sugar

¼ cup (60 ml) apple cider vinegar

2 tablespoons (28 ml) Worcestershire sauce (I use Bear & Burton's Fireshire.)

1 tablespoon (14 g) garlic paste

1 teaspoon garlic powder

1 teaspoon onion powder

1. Prepare the smoker with hickory wood, heated to about 300°F (150°C).

2. Pat the rib racks dry and then coat in the sweet and spicy sauce. Dust liberally with the rub. Smoke the ribs for about 3 hours or until the internal temperature reaches 195°F (91°C).

3. In a large cast-iron pot or saucepan over medium heat, combine the whiskey sauce ingredients and bring to a vigorous boil while stirring constantly. Reduce to a gentle boil, just above a simmer, and reduce the sauce down to about 1⅓ cups (315 ml) of liquid. Transfer to a Mason jar and set aside.

4. When the ribs reach 195°F (91°C), coat them with the whiskey sauce and smoke for 10 minutes more. Let them rest for about 20 minutes before slicing and serving with the rest of the sauce on the side.

BUFFALO RIBS ON STEROIDS

YIELD: 4 to 6 servings — PREP: 30 minutes — COOK: 3 hours

Yeah, succulent ribs are all the bomb. You'll get there with this recipe thanks to long smoking time and some pure-gold rub. But what a lot of home cooks and even veteran Pitmasters forget is that contrast adds interest, especially when it comes to eating BBQ. For every super spicy blend, it's wise to have something creamy to mellow things out and offer a little relief. And for every fall-off-the-bone tender rack of ribs that have been smoked to perfection with spices that elevate the rich meat flavor, it's nice to have some crunch and resistance to the bite. That's why I like to use everything bagel seasoning. It's a small thing, but it adds more than you would think. Always give a little thought to contrast in the flavors and textures of whatever you grill, smoke, or cook.

For the Ribs

3 racks (2 pounds, or 910 g each) baby back ribs

¼ cup (60 ml) olive oil

½ cup (96 g) spicy BBQ rub (I use Blazing Star Reaper Rub and Seasoning.)

½ cup (96 g) all-purpose seasoning (I use Blazing Star All in One Seasoning.)

For the Buffalo Sauce

½ cup (120 ml) avocado oil

1 head garlic, peeled and minced

2 tablespoons (8 g) chili flakes

2 tablespoons (24 g) everything bagel seasoning

2–3 tablespoons (32–48 g) BBQ sauce (I use [35–53 g] Blazing Star Original BBQ Sauce.)

1 cup (235 ml) buffalo wing sauce

2 tablespoons (24 g) spicy BBQ rub (I use Blazing Star Reaper Rub and Seasoning.)

8 tablespoons (4 ounces, or 112 g) salted butter

1. Prepare the smoker with hickory wood, heated to about 350°F (180°C).

2. Coat the ribs on both sides with the olive oil and dust them generously with the rub and seasoning blend. Smoke the ribs for about 3 hours or until the internal temperature reaches 160°F (71°C) and the ribs are nicely charred. Let rest for 20 minutes.

3. While the ribs rest, make the sauce. In a 4-quart (3.8 L) saucepot over medium heat, combine the sauce ingredients and stir until the butter is completely melted and incorporated and the sauce is slightly thickened.

4. Cut the racks into individual ribs and transfer them to a large bowl. Dress generously with the sauce and serve.

SMOKED AND AIR-FRIED GARLIC STICKY RIBS

YIELD: 3 to 4 servings — PREP: 30 minutes — COOK: 2½ hours

Mostly it's about the food; but sometimes, it's about the tool. I love the garlic-heavy flavors of these ribs, and the salty-sweet vibe. More than that, though? I'm all in on taking advantage of the latest in grilling technology—the combination grill, smoker, and air fryer. I love mine, and it's worth considering buying your own, especially if you like to mix up cooking methods and do a lot of outdoor BBQ feasts. This combo smoker is incredibly handy as an all-in-one go-to for grilling, smoking, and air frying. The ribs in this dish are proof positive you won't miss a beat flavor-wise.

For the Ribs

1 rack (1½ pounds, or 680 g) pork spareribs

2 tablespoons (28 ml) olive oil

2 tablespoons (36 g) salt

2 tablespoons (12 g) coarse ground black pepper

2 tablespoons (18 g) garlic powder

For the Sauce

4 tablespoons (55 g) unsalted butter

1 tablespoon (10 g) minced garlic

1 cup (235 ml) sweet chili sauce

1 tablespoon (15 ml) soy sauce

Crispy fried garlic (optional)

1. Pat the ribs dry and then coat with the olive oil. Whisk together the salt, pepper, and garlic powder (you can use an SPG mix if you have one) and thoroughly dust both sides of the ribs. Pat to ensure the spices adhere.

2. Place the ribs in the combo smoker. Fill the smoking chamber with an all-purpose blend of wood pellets. Set to the smoker setting and dial in the heat to 250°F (120°C). Smoke the ribs for 2 hours, turning them after 1 hour.

3. Slice the ribs and return to the combo smoker set on air fry. Set the heat to 390°F (199°C) and air fry the ribs for 20 minutes.

4. In a large cast-iron skillet over medium heat, melt the butter. Add the garlic and cook until fragrant. Add the chili and soy sauces and cook for 5 minutes more.

5. Transfer the ribs to a large bowl. Pour the sauce over the ribs and mix until thoroughly coated. Plate the ribs and garnish with crispy fried garlic, if desired.

CHICHARRON PORK BELLY

YIELD: 4 servings — PREP: 1 hour — REFRIGERATION: 24 hours — COOK: 3½ hours

Spend a little time in the Philippines and you're likely to come across a version of this dish. Chicharron roughly translates to "crackling" and is traditionally fried pork rinds. Filipinos eat chicharron (they sometimes call it tsitsaron) as a bar snack, and you can even pick some up in small neighborhood convenience stores. There are lots of ways to make chicharron, and a lot of different tropical flavors can be used (just about every island nation has their own version). I love pork belly because it has some of the richest flavor of any BBQ cut, so I go extremely simple with my version. Prepare it right, with just a little spritz of lime, and there will be angels dancing on your tongue.

2 pounds (910 g) pork belly, skin on

3 tablespoons (36 g) beef rub (I use Blazing Star Beef Rub and Seasoning.)

½ cup (112 g) kosher salt

1 large lime, halved

1. Pat the meat dry and season the meat side of the pork belly with the beef rub. Pat to ensure the rub adheres to the meat.

2. Use the blade of a knife to scrape the skin side repeatedly until you have removed the top layer of moisture. Refrigerate uncovered overnight to dry out the skin.

3. Prepare the smoker with applewood, heated to 250°F (120°C). Coat the skin side of the pork belly with a thick layer of kosher salt.

4. Smoke the pork belly in indirect heat for 2 to 3 hours or until the fat begins to render. Remove the pork belly, scrape the salt off the skin, and return the pork to the smoker.

5. Increase the heat as high as possible to crisp the skin. (If your smoker has a top rack, add hot coals to an aluminum tray and place it above the pork belly.) Smoke until the skin bubbles and crisps.

6. Let the pork belly rest for 15 to 30 minutes. Slice, cube, and serve, spritzed with fresh lime juice.

SPICY PORK BELLY BURNT ENDS

YIELD: 4 to 6 servings — PREP: 30 minutes — COOK: 4 hours

There are two reasons I absolutely love pork belly and making it as burnt ends. First, you really don't need to do much for an amazing taste sensation. This particular cut is rich, dense, and filthy with flavor-rich fat. And two, burnt ends allow maximum coverage of whatever spices you choose to use. Every single bite you take of these is going to be as smack-you-in-the-face delicious as the last one. This is an ideal recipe because it is just about impossible to mess up, and everyone at the cookout is going to think you're a BBQ god.

3 pounds (1.4 kg) pork belly, skin on

½ cup (96 g) extra spicy BBQ rub (I use Blazing Star Scorpion Rub and Seasoning.)

1 cup (235 ml) apple juice

4 tablespoons (55 g) unsalted butter

½ cup (125 g) BBQ sauce (I use Blazing Star Spicy BBQ Sauce.)

2 large jalapeños

1. Prepare the smoker with the wood of your choice, heated to 250°F (120°C).

2. Cut the pork belly into 1-inch (2.5 cm) cubes. Coat the cubes all over with the rub. Transfer them to a wire rack and smoke them for 2 hours. Transfer the apple juice to a spray bottle and spray the cubes every 30 minutes.

3. After 2 hours, transfer the pork belly cubes to an aluminum roasting pan. Top with the butter and half the BBQ sauce. Toss well until the cubes are completely coated all over.

4. Tightly cover the pan with aluminum foil, place it in the smoker, and smoke for 1½ hours more.

5. Remove the foil and coat the cubes with the remaining BBQ sauce. Return the pan to the smoker uncovered and smoke for 30 minutes.

6. Thinly slice the jalapeños and garnish each cube with one slice. Serve and enjoy!

HONEY BUFFALO PORK BELLY BURNT ENDS

YIELD: 4 servings — PREP: 15 minutes — COOK: 2 hours

You might have noticed throughout this book that I sometimes specify certain name-brand products. It's not because I have stock in those companies (although, not a bad idea—I'm going to think on that!), it's because I lean heavy on certain ingredients that hit the ball out of the park. If it ain't broke, why fix it? That's the case in this sweet-savory recipe, where I use one of my very favorite Buffalo BBQ sauces. I urge you to find your own favorites and let them do some of the heavy lifting for you. There's no need to reinvent the wheel every time.

2 pounds (910 g) pork belly, skin on

½ cup (96 g) extra spicy BBQ rub (I use Blazing Star Scorpion Rub and Seasoning.)

½ cup (120 g) buffalo sauce (I use Tacticalories HELLDIVER Buffalo Wing Sauce.)

8 tablespoons (112 g) unsalted butter

¼ cup (80 g) cup hot or plain honey (I use Mike's Hot Honey.)

2 tablespoons (24 g) everything bagel seasoning

1. Prepare the smoker with applewood, heated to about 250°F (120°C).

2. Cut the pork belly into 1-inch (2.5 cm) cubes and transfer to a large bowl. Sprinkle with the rub and mix thoroughly by hand until all the cubes are completely coated. Transfer the cubes to a wire rack. Smoke the pork belly for 2 hours.

3. Transfer the cubes to an aluminum roasting pan. Drizzle with the buffalo wing sauce. Cut the butter into four pieces and add to the pan. Toss the pork belly cubes until the butter is melted and each cube is completely coated. Tightly cover the pan with a large sheet of aluminum foil and place the pan in the smoker.

4. Smoke the pork for 1 to 2 hours more or until tender to a probe and the internal temperature reaches about 200°F (93°C).

5. Drizzle the smoked pork with about half the hot honey and return to the smoker for 15 minutes more.

6. Remove and let cool for 5 to 10 minutes or until the cubes can be handled. Drizzle with the remaining hot honey and sprinkle with the everything bagel seasoning. Serve and enjoy!

ASIAN BANG BRISKET BURNT ENDS

YIELD: 4 servings — PREP: 30 minutes — COOK: 8 hours

Do you like Szechuan takeout and pork dishes? Then you're going to love this smoked treasure. I turned to an Asian-style BBQ sauce for a little bit of the authentic Szechuan spice explosion and tempered it with a healthy dose of my favorite beer. You can try to create that signature Szechuan flavor from scratch, but I think that's setting yourself up for failure. This is a case where using an existing product off the shelf is going to serve you—and the recipe—better. Trust me, your taste buds will thank you.

1 brisket (2 pounds, or 910 g)

3 tablespoons (45 ml) olive oil

¼ cup (48 g) charcoal BBQ rub (I use RubCity Date Night.)

½ cup (140 g) Asian BBQ sauce (I use Blazing Star Asian Bang Sauce.)

½ can or bottle (6 ounces, or 177 ml) pale ale (I use Firestone Walker 805 California Blonde Ale.)

2 tablespoons (24 g) everything bagel seasoning

1. Prepare the smoker with your preferred wood, heated to 250°F (120°C).

2. Cut the brisket into 1-inch (2.5 cm) cubes. Transfer the cubes to a large aluminum roasting pan and drizzle with the olive oil. Toss until the cubes are completely coated and then dust liberally with the charcoal BBQ rub and toss again until all the meat is evenly coated.

3. Place the cubes on a wire rack and smoke for 3 to 4 hours or until the surface is charred and crusty.

4. Drizzle the cubes with about half of the Asian BBQ sauce. Toss to coat and then add the beer to the pan and toss the cubes in the beer. Tightly cover with a large sheet of aluminum foil. Place the pan in the smoker and smoke for 4 hours or until the meat is fall-apart tender.

5. Uncover the pan, toss the meat in the juices, and leave in the smoker uncovered for another 15 minutes to get an extra crispy surface.

6. Dress the smoked cubes with the remaining Asian BBQ sauce and dust with the everything bagel seasoning before serving.

TOMAHAWK STEAK WITH JALAPEÑO GARLIC CREAM SAUCE

YIELD: 4 servings —— PREP: 10 minutes —— COOK: 60 minutes

There is just something about cooking over an open firepit. It's like being a cowboy on the open range or living a rough-and-ready life out in the tundra. Fire is fire, but meat cooked over a pit comes away with a special type of flavor. Of course, only certain cuts are right for open-pit cooking. The absolute best is a tomahawk steak. The steak itself is delicious plain and especially when finished quickly on the grill. But add a cream sauce and wow! Creamy, cheesy richness is just the ideal contrast to that simple, deep, meaty flavor. The combination is going to rock your BBQ world.

For the Steak

1 tomahawk steak (1½–2 pounds, or 680–910 g)

¼ cup (60 ml) Worcestershire sauce (I use Bear & Burton's W Sauce.)

3 tablespoons (36 g) beef rub of choice

For the Sauce

4 tablespoons (55 g) salted butter

6 cloves garlic, peeled and minced

1 jalapeño, diced

2 tablespoons (16 g) all-purpose flour

1 cup (235 ml) beef broth, plus more as needed

1 teaspoon dried basil

½ teaspoon dried oregano

½ cup (120 ml) heavy cream, plus more as needed

½ cup (50 g) freshly grated Parmesan cheese

1 ounce (28 g) cream cheese, room temperature

Kosher salt and freshly ground black pepper to taste

(CONTINUED)

1. Prepare a firepit with almond or oak wood.

2. Coat the steak all over with the Worcestershire sauce. Season liberally with the beef rub. Drill a hole in the bone and hang the steak over the firepit. Cook the steak for about 2 hours or until the internal temperature reaches 120°F (49°C).

3. Finish the steak by searing it on a grill for 3 to 5 minutes or until the internal temperature reaches 130°F (54°C). Remove the steak and let it rest for 5 to 10 minutes.

4. While the steak rests, make the sauce. In a large cast-iron skillet over medium-high heat, melt the butter. Add the garlic and jalapeño and cook until fragrant, 1 to 2 minutes. Whisk in the flour and cook until lightly browned, about 1 minute. Add the beef broth, basil, and oregano. Cook, whisking constantly, until the ingredients are entirely incorporated, 1 to 2 minutes.

5. Stir in the heavy cream, Parmesan, and cream cheese. Keep stirring until the sauce has thickened slightly, 1 to 2 minutes. If the sauce becomes too thick, add more beef broth or heavy cream. Season with salt and pepper to taste.

6. Cut the steak into thick slices. Spoon a generous amount of the sauce over the slices and serve.

PICANHA AND HABANERO CHIMICHURRI SANDWICH

YIELD: 4 to 6 servings — PREP: 40 minutes — COOK: 2½ hours

If you've never worked with picanha, you've missed out. It's a Brazilian cut offered as either a steak or a roast. I like to work with the roast, sometimes sold as "cap of rump." The roast is perfectly marbled with fat, which translates to incredibly tender and flavorful meat. Surprisingly, it's also a really affordable cut and an inexpensive way to fill a lot of stomachs. Picanha is fantastic on its own, but really comes to life in a sandwich. For this one, I've combined soft and chewy ciabatta rolls with the slightly tangy bite of melted provolone and a memorable chimichurri sauce. This is one of those dishes that you'll have hard time not taking seconds, even when you're full.

For the Picanha Roast

1 picanha roast (3–3¼ pounds, or 1.4–1.5 kg)

2 tablespoons (28 ml) olive oil

½ cup (96 g) beef rub of choice

For the Habanero Chimichurri

½ cup (120 ml) olive oil, plus more as needed

2 habanero peppers, diced

1 head garlic, peeled and minced

1 small shallot, peeled and diced

1 cup (60 g) chopped fresh parsley

1 cup (16 g) chopped cilantro

Zest and juice of 1 lime

1 tablespoon (14 g) kosher salt

1 tablespoon (8 g) coarse ground black pepper

1 tablespoon (4 g) crushed red pepper flakes

¼ cup (60 ml) red wine vinegar

For Serving

1 wheel (8 ounces, or 225 g) provolone cheese

4–6 ciabatta rolls

(CONTINUED)

1. Prepare the smoker with hickory wood, heated to about 350°F (180°C).

2. Coat the picanha in olive oil and then dust with the beef rub. Smoke for about 1 hour, turning the roast midway through, until the internal temperature reaches 125°F (52°C). Remove and cover the roast with a large sheet of aluminum foil. Let it rest for 20 to 30 minutes.

3. While the picanha is resting, make the chimichurri. In a small cast-iron pot over medium-high heat, heat the oil. Add the habanero peppers and garlic and cook for 1 to 2 minutes or until fragrant. Add the remaining ingredients, stirring until thickened slightly (add more olive oil to thin the sauce if needed).

4. In a cast-iron skillet over low heat, melt the provolone wheel until gooey and crispy on top. Set aside.

5. Cut the picanha into thin slices. Line the bottom of a ciabatta roll with a double layer of the slices and top with a big dollop of the melted provolone. Scoop a heaping spoonful of Habanero Chimichurri over the cheese and finish with the ciabatta top half. Repeat with the remaining ingredients, serve, and enjoy!

SMOKED CHILEAN SEA BASS

WITH GARLIC BROWN BUTTER

YIELD: 2 servings — PREP: 10 minutes — COOK: 45 minutes

Sometimes called Patagonian toothfish, Chilean sea bass is one of the most impressive fish I've ever cooked. It is silky on the tongue, with a naturally sweet, almost buttery flavor. Smoked over applewood, it flakes up and the abundant natural oils guarantee that the fish won't dry out. That gives you the chance to put a nice crust on the white flesh. I cook mine on cedar planks, which is the way I think most fish should be smoked.

2 pounds (910 g) Chilean sea bass

3 tablespoons (45 ml) olive oil, divided

2 tablespoons (24 g) garlic butter rub (I use Boars Night Out White Lightning Double Garlic Butter Barbecue Seasoning.)

1 tablespoon (8 g) freshly ground black pepper

6 tablespoons (85 g) unsalted butter

2 tablespoons (20 g) minced garlic

1. Prepare the smoker with applewood and your favorite charcoal (I use Jealous Devil Maxx XL Charcoal Briquettes), heated to 350°F (180°C).

2. Coat the sea bass with 2 tablespoons (28 ml) of olive oil. Season with the rub and dust with the freshly ground black pepper. Oil a soaked cedar plank with the remaining olive oil and place the sea bass in the center of the plank.

3. Smoke in indirect heat until the rub has formed a crispy crust or until the internal temperature reaches 127°F (53°C). Remove and set aside until the carryover cooking has raised the internal temperature to 130°F (54°C).

4. In the meantime, remove the deflector plate, if any. Place a large cast-iron skillet over the smoker coals. Add the butter and stir constantly until the milk solids brown. Add the garlic and cook until it also browns.

5. Pour the sauce over the sea bass and then cut into individual portions and serve.

REVERSE-SEARED DUCK BREAST

YIELD: 2 servings — PREP: 10 minutes — COOK: 3 hours

Here is an entirely new tool in your BBQ arsenal, one that may take a little time but delivers unequaled results. Reverse searing is perfect for duck breast because the point is to create a crustlike char on the outside, while keeping the inside tender, delicate, and ultra juicy. That's all-important with duck breast because it's a meat like no other. There is a sweet, otherworldly flavor to duck, and you want all of it in the final serving. The process of reverse searing gives you incredible control, and I recommend you shoot for medium-rare to make the most of the duck breast flavor and texture. It's such a special meat that I season it simply, with little more than salt and pepper. Anything other than that is like plating gold in silver; there's just no reason to.

1 duck breast (2 pounds, or 910 g), skin on

¼ cup (72 g) sea salt

2 tablespoons (16 g) freshly ground black pepper

2 tablespoons (18 g) garlic powder

2 tablespoons (28 ml) olive oil

1 tablespoon (12 g) sriracha sea salt (I use Osmo Flakey Sriracha Sea Salt.)

1. Prepare the smoker with your wood of choice, heated to 225°F (107°C).

2. Crosshatch the duck breast skin in a diamond pattern. Score deeply, but don't cut into the meat. Season liberally with sea salt. Flip the breast and season the meat side with the remaining salt, pepper, and garlic powder.

3. Smoke the duck breast for 2½ to 3 hours or until the internal temperature reaches 115°F (46°C).

4. Grease a large, cold, cast-iron pan with the olive oil and set the duck breast in the pan skin-side down. Cook over medium heat until the fat renders, the skin is crispy, and the internal temperature reaches 125°F to 130°F (52°C to 54°C).

5. Remove the duck breast and let it rest for 10 to 15 minutes or until the internal temperature reaches 130°F to 135°F (54°C to 57°C).

6. Slice the breast, dust with the sriracha sea salt, and serve juicy and hot.

SMOKED STUFFED BELL PEPPERS

YIELD: 6 servings — PREP: 15 minutes — COOK: 30 minutes

Stuffed bell peppers are that kind of family standby that's been a last-minute dinner idea for busy parents dating all the way back to about the 1950s. Don't get me wrong; it's an okay meal even if, as a kid, you weren't exactly thrilled to see it on your plate. I decided it really needed updating with a fresh blast of meaty flavor and smoky goodness. The secret to the reinvention? A triple-meat combo with some of the best spice blends ever to see the topside of a grill. The taco meat package I use includes pollo asado, beef carne asada, and sausage al pastor. It turns the humble stuffed pepper into a flavor explosion and something special for the dinner table.

1 package (3 pounds, or 1.4 kg) Calle Sabor Street Taco Cart

3 cups (558 g) cooked rice, divided

1 large red bell pepper

1 large yellow bell pepper

1 large green bell pepper

2 tablespoons (28 ml) olive oil

Salt and pepper to tase

1 package (8 ounces, or 225 g) sharp cheddar cheese (or substitute packaged shredded cheese)

2 tablespoons (24 g) BBQ rub of choice

2 tablespoons (35 g) BBQ sauce

1. Prepare the smoker with hickory wood, heated to medium or about 300°F (150°C).

2. In a large pan over medium-high heat, break up the pollo asado. When browned and cooked through, add 1 cup (186 g) of the rice and stir until combined. Set aside. Repeat with the carne asada and al pastor meats.

3. Cut each bell pepper in half from top to bottom. Seed and clean each half. Arrange them on a sheet pan or baking sheet. Grease the inside of each pepper half with olive oil. Season with salt and pepper to taste.

4. Fill each color of bell pepper with a different meat. Press the meat and rice mixtures firmly into the halves. Shred the cheese over each half to create a thick top layer. Press the cheese firmly onto each bell pepper half. Dust with BBQ rub.

5. Smoke for about 30 minutes or until the cheese is melted and creates a crust and the peppers are soft. Remove, drizzle with BBQ sauce, and serve.

SMOKED SALMON CHOWDER

YIELD: 6 to 8 servings — PREP: 20 minutes — COOK: 45 minutes to 1 hour

*No knock on New England and its clams, but this is a whole nother level of chowder.
The creamy base was always begging to be cut with some sharp Cajun heat, and salmon is a
more complex flavor than the traditional shellfish. You can go even hotter by substituting habaneros
for the jalapeños. But try this version first because the heat is what I would call high-medium and right
in the sweet spot for most people. No matter what, though, this is the perfect filling meal in a
bowl for cold nights by the Bay or anywhere, really.*

1 salmon steak (1½ pounds, or 680 g), skin removed and cut into 1-inch (2.5 cm) pieces

2 tablespoons (24 g) Cajun rub of choice

4 tablespoons (55 g) unsalted butter

½ pound (225 g) bacon, cut into ½-inch (1.3 cm) pieces

3 stalks celery, diced

1 small onion, peeled and minced

2 jalapeños, sliced thin with the seeds (reserve some for garnish)

1 bunch scallions, finely chopped (reserve some for garnish)

1 head garlic, peeled and minced

4 cups (945 ml) chicken stock (or substitute seafood stock)

2 large russet potatoes, peeled and cut into 1-inch (2.5 cm) pieces

1 tablespoon (18 g) salt

1 tablespoon (6 g) freshly ground black pepper

1-2 tablespoons (8-16 g) cornstarch

1-2 tablespoons (15-30 ml) water

2 cups (255 g) frozen whole-kernel corn

2 cups (475 ml) heavy cream

(CONTINUED)

1. Prepare the smoker with applewood to a low heat, around 225°F (107°C). You want the salmon to just absorb the smoke, not fully cook.

2. In a large bowl, carefully coat the salmon with the Cajun rub. Transfer to a baking sheet (to catch the juices). Smoke the fish until it reaches an internal temperature of 90°F to 100°F (32°C to 38°C), about 45 minutes to 1 hour.

3. While the salmon is smoking, melt the butter in a large pot over medium heat. Add the bacon and cook until crispy. Remove the bacon and set aside.

4. Add the celery, onions, jalapeños, scallions, and garlic to the pot. Cook until softened.

5. Add the stock, potatoes, salt, and pepper. Return the bacon to the pot. Bring the mixture to a simmer and cook until the potatoes are tender, about 15 minutes.

6. Mix the cornstarch with just enough water to make a slurry. Add the slurry to the pot, stir in, and bring to boil. Boil until the mixture is thickened slightly. Reduce the heat to a simmer. Add the corn and heavy cream.

7. Gently add the smoked salmon. Carefully stir the chowder to avoid breaking the salmon pieces. Cover and simmer for 10 minutes more or until the salmon is cooked through.

8. Top with the bacon and reserved scallions and jalapeños. Serve hot and enjoy!

RESOURCES

Al Frugoni
alfrugoni.com
There are some great rubs over here; I use their Chimichurri The Original, but they have others, too.

Alpine Butcher
alpinebutcher.com
These guys do some great Wagyu cuts.

Avid Armor
avidarmor.com
I'm the proud owner of the Avid Armor Ultra Series Model USV32 Chamber Vacuum Sealer and use it a lot on the marinade function to infuse meat and poultry with unmatched flavor.

Bear & Burton's Old Florida Sauce Co.
thewsauce.com
I use their W Sauce or Fireshire instead of Worcestershire sauce in a lot of my beef recipes. They have a lot of other sauces that are worth a try as well.

Blazing Star BBQ
blazingstarbbq.com
I'm all in on their Reaper Rub & Seasoning spice mix, but they have other dynamite sauces and rubs, too.

Boars Night Out
boarsnightout.com
These guys offer three different unique rubs, along with a list of places you can pick them up.

Cacique
caciquefoods.com
Grab some of their crema Mexicana to use as a dressing or dip.

Campo Grande
eatcampogrande.com
They sell pork-and-beef blends you might have a hard time finding locally—and in bulk.

Char-Griller
chargriller.com
Hit them up for a great grill, griddle, or parts—all on the same website (or available through retailers). I'm a fan of the Gravity Fed 980.

Chuds BBQ
chudsbbq.com
I regularly use their SPG seasoning, and their Chud Box is one of my favorite direct-fire grills.

Fresh Vintage Farms
freshvintagefarms.com
The company offers premium nut oils as alternatives to olive oil. It's a cool way to add different flavors to sauces and marinades.

Fyr
fyr.com
They sell different types of hot sauces for just about any BBQ dish you can imagine.

Gold Bar Whiskey

goldbarwhiskey.com
They make a unique blended whiskey of corn mash with a touch of rye, perfect for whiskey BBQ bastes and sauces.

Jealous Devil

jealousdevil.com
This is my go-to for charcoal.

Kinder's

kinders.com
You'll love the Bourbon Peach Wing Sauce & Dip, but they also sell a whole shelf of rubs, sauces, and seasonings.

King's Hawaiian

kingshawaiian.com
I like their Original Hawaiian Sweet Rolls for sliders, but they sell other buns and sauces as well. It's all delicious.

Meat Church

meatchurch.com
I like to use their Honey Hog BBQ Rub on cuts of pork.

Meat District

eatmeatdistrict.com
They sell premium Angus meats, including my go-to burger patty, THE SHAQ Premium Burger.

Meater

meater.com
Meater sells thermometers specifically for barbecuing and grilling. They build quality thermometers that are durable and easy to use, which is why I always have one nearby.

Melinda's Hot Sauces

melindas.com
Here you'll find a selection of high-quality hot sauces, wing sauces, and dipping sauces.

Miller Lite

millerlite.com
This is my go-to beer.

Mike's Hot Honey

mikeshothoney.com
They sell two versions of their honey—hot and extra hot. I like to use it in my Cajun smoked recipes, but these honeys are also great for cocktails or just to use as condiment.

Ninja

ninjakitchen.com
They sell the Ninja Woodfire Outdoor Grill, a combination grill, smoker, and air fryer that is pretty much the Swiss Army knife of barbecuing equipment.

Nomad

nomadgrills.com
Want to get knee-deep in specialty grills, griddles, and accessories? Look no further than Nomad. They offer the best portable grill on the market.

Osmo

osmosalt.com
These next-level salts will change the way you think about the simplest of seasonings. I lean heavy on their Flakey White Sea Salt.

Pinky Poppin' Umami

gustusvitae.com

Check out my good friend Chuck's Flavor Trains seasoning collaboration. Gustus Vitae distributes Flavor Train rubs and seasonings (along with some cool flavored salts), including Pinky Poppin Umami—5th Taste Flavor BBQ Rub. I use their line of Bougie BBQ rubs.

RC Ranch

r-cranch.com

They offer a wide selection of high-quality American Wagyu meat from Texas.

RubCity

rubcity.com

They have rubs and seasonings for every occasion and every meal.

Strongarm Bar & Grill

strongarmbarandgrill.com

They sell many great seasonings and sauces.

Super Skewers

superskewer.com

The right skewers can make a dish much easier to prepare. I use Super Skewers, which have two prongs and a sturdy construction that can hold even a heavy load of meat. These things will last forever, so they're an investment.

Tacticalories Seasoning Company

tacticalories.com

Seasonings, salsas, sauces, and more make this a must-visit online store for any aspiring Pitmaster.

Tagwood BBQ

tagwoodbbq.com

They manufacture one of my very favorite Argentine-style open-fire grills.

Terrapin Ridge Farms

terrapinridge.com

They have a huge selection of flavored jams, including my favorite: Hot Habanero Bacon Jam!

Tony Chachere

tonychachere.com

This site is packed with justly famous Creole Cajun seasonings and sauces.

Truff

truff.com

This here is just truffle oil done right.

Wild Fork Foods

wildforkfoods.com

They sell a full range of meats, including some cuts you might not be able to find locally.

Zarlengo Seasoning

zarlengoseasoning.com

You'll find just great Italian seasoning right here.

ACKNOWLEDGMENTS

Thank you: To everyone who had a hand in helping with this book. To my mother and father for shaping me into the cook I am today. To my wife, Mellissa, for being the backbone of everything in my life. To my children, whom I love so much and do all of this for. To my BBQ family for inspiring me to be the best at what we do. To my friend, Carlos Bradley, for taking the time out of his super busy schedule to help shoot all these amazing photos. To all my partners, collaborators, sponsors, family, and friends who have been an integral part of my journey over the past few years—your unwavering support, creativity, and friendship have made this adventure not only successful but truly memorable. Together, we've achieved so much, and I'm excited to continue building on these strong relationships in the future. Thank you for being an essential part of this incredible chapter in my life.

ABOUT THE AUTHOR

Tony Ramirez, also known as TFTI BBQ on social media, has spent nearly twenty years perfecting his backyard barbecue skills in the Bay Area of California. Born in Charleston, South Carolina, Tony is self-taught, inspired by his Filipino and Cajun heritage, his beloved parents, and a passion for *BBQ Pitmasters* reruns, YouTube tutorials, and personal culinary experiments. What started in 2021 as a hobby of posting BBQ pictures and videos has since evolved into a full-time career, with Tony partnering with major brands like Miller Lite, Char-Griller, Reynolds Brands, and Tony Chachere's. His unique, approachable flavor combinations and techniques, which sometimes bend traditional barbecue "rules," have earned him a beloved spot in the live-fire BBQ community. Find him online on all major social media platforms as TFTI BBQ.

INDEX